D0983975

# THE WRITINGS OF MARSHALL McLUHAN

and

What has been written about him

A Bibliography

# THE WRITINGS OF MARSHALL McLUHAN

Listed in chronological order

from 1934 to 1975

with an appended list of reviews
and articles about him and his
work.

Wake-Brook House

BOOK PUBLISHERS

## HERBERT MARSHALL McLUHAN

Born: Edmonton, Alberta, Canada. 7283 - 15 - 173

University of Manitoba — B.A. 1932: M.A. 1934.
Cambridge University — B.A. 1936: M.A. 1939: Ph.D. 1942.
Full Professor — 1952.

Taught at the University of Wisconsin — 1936-1937.
Taught at the University of St. Louis — 1937-1944.
Taught at Assumption University — 1944-1946.
Taught at St. Michael's College, University of Toronto — 1946 to
        present.

Chairman of Ford Foundation Seminar on Culture and
        Communication — 1953-1955.

Co-editor of "Explorations Magazine" — 1954-1959.

Director of Media project for National Association of Educational
        Broadcasters, and Office of Education, U.S.A.
        1959-1960.

Fellow of the Royal Society of Canada — 1964.

Appointment in 1963 by the President of the University of
        Toronto to create new Center for Culture and
        Technology (to study the psychic and social
        consequences of technologies and media).

Married Corinne Lewis of Fort Worth, Texas, 1939.

Honorary Degrees received from each of the following
        institutions:

| University of Windsor | 1965 — D.Litt. |
| Assumption University | 1966 — D.Litt. |
| University of Manitoba | 1967 — D.Litt. |
| Simon Fraser University | 1967 — LL.D. |
| Grinnell University, Iowa | 1967 — D.Litt. |
| St. John Fisher College | 1969 — Lit.Hum. |
| University of Alberta | 1971 — LL.D. |
| Univ. of Western Ontario | 1972 — D.Litt. |
| University of Toronto | 1977 — D.Litt. |

Received Honorary Award in Culture and Communications from
        Niagara University, New York 1967.

Molson Award for outstanding achievement in the Social
Sciences, 1967.

Appointment to the Schweitzer Chair in the Humanities,
Fordham University, New York, 1967-1968.

Appointment as a Companion of the Order of Canada, 1970.

Received The Institute of Public Relations President's Award
(Great Britain) 1970.

Received The Christian Culture Award, Assumption University,
1971.

Received Citation from The Religious Educational Association
of the United States and Canada, 1973.

Received Civic Award of Merit from Mayor David Crombie at
Toronto City Hall, 1974.

Received "Man of Achievement" Diploma from the International Biographical Centre, Cambridge, England,
1975.

Appointment to the McDermott Chair at the University of
Dallas, Irving, Texas, from April 10 to May 10, 1975.

Outstanding Lectures:
Second Annual A.V.B. Geoghegan Lecture, University of
Pennsylvania, 1966.
Marfleet Lectures, University of Toronto, 1967.
Purves Memorial Lecture, American Institute of Architects,
New York, 1967.
Congressional Breakfast, Washington, D.C., 1970.
Gillett Lecture Series, University of Western Ontario, 1970.
Mary C. Richardson Lecture, State University College of
Arts and Science, Geneseo, New York, 1970.
McAuley Lecture, St. Joseph College, West Hartford,
Connecticut, 1972.
Gerstein Lecture Series, York University, Toronto, 1975.

Gold Medal Award from President of the Italian Republic at
Rimini, Italy, in recognition of original work as
philosopher of the mass media, 1971.

President's Cabinet Award, University of Detroit, 1972.

Vatican appointment as consultor of the Pontifical Commission
for Social Communications, 1973.

# The Writings Of Marshall McLuhan

**934**    *George Meredith as a Poet and Dramatic Parodist,* M.A. Thesis, University of Manitoba.

**936**    "G. K. Chesterton: a practical mystic," *Dalhousie Review,* Vol. 15, pp. 455-64.

**937**    "The Cambridge English School," *Fleur De Lis,* St. Louis University, pp. 21-25.

"The Non-Being of Non-Being"

"Creative Thought vs. Pragmatism"

"Apes and Angels" — *Fleur De Lis,* St. Louis University, December, 1937. pp. 7-9.

**1938**    "Peter or Peter Pan," *Fleur De Lis,* St. Louis University (date and volume number not known) pp. 4-7.

**1943**    *The Place of Thomas Nashe in the Learning of His Time* — Ph.D. Thesis, Cambridge University.

"Aesthetic Patterns in Keats' Odes" — *University of Toronto Quarterly,* Volume 12, No. 2, January, 1943. pp. 167-179.

"Education of Free Men in Democracy: The Liberal Arts" — *St. Louis University Studies in Honour of St. Thomas Aquinas,* Volume 1, pp. 47-50.

"Herbert's Virtue" — *The Explicator,* Volume 1, #2, October, 1943. (Reprinted in *Readings For Liberal Education,* L. G. Locke, W. M. Gibson & G. Arms, eds., New York: Rinehart 1948, pp. 534-535.)

**1944**    "Dagwood's America" — *Columbia,* Volume 23, January, 1944, pp. 3 and 22.

"Henley's Invictus" — *Explicator,* Vol. 3, December, 1944, #22.

"Edgar Poe's Tradition" — *Sewanee Review,* Volume 52, #1, January, 1944, pp. 24-33.

"Eliot's 'The Hippopotamus'" — *The Explicator,* Volume 2, #7, May, 1944.

"Kipling and Forster"—*Sewanee Review*, Volume 52, #3, July, 1944, pp. 332-343.

"Wyndham Lewis: Lemuel in Lilliput"—*St. Louis University Studies in Honour of St. Thomas Aquinas*, Volume 2, 1944, pp. 58-72.

"Poetic vs. Rhetorical Exegesis, *Sewanee Review*, Volume 52, #2, April, 1944, pp. 266-76.

1945   "The Analogical Mirrors"—*Gerard Manley Hopkins*, Kenyon Critics Edition, New Direction Books, Norfolk, Connecticut, 1945, pp. 15-27. (Reprinted in *Hopkins*, G. H. Hartman, ed. 1966.)

"The New York Wits"—*Kenyon Review*, Volume 7, #1, 1945, pp. 12-28.

"Another Aesthetic Peep-Show"—*Sewanee Review*, #53, Autumn, 1945, pp. 674-676.

1946   "An Ancient Quarrel in Modern America"—*The Classical Journal*, Volume 41, #4 (January, 1946) pp. 156-62.

"Footprints in the Sands of Crime"—*Sewanee Review*, Volume 54, #4, October, 1946, pp. 617-34.

"Out of the Castle Into the Counting-House"—*Politics*, pp. 227-79.

1947   "American Advertising"—*Horizon*, #93-94, pp. 132-41.

"Inside Blake and Hollywood"—*Sewanee Review*, Volume 55, October, 1947, pp. 710-15.

"Mr. Connelly and Mr. Hook"—*Sewanee Review*, Volume 55, #1, July, 1947, pp. 167-72.

*Introduction* to *Paradox in Chesterton* by Hugh Kenner, New York: Sheed and Ward, 1947 (pp. xi-xxii)

"The Southern Quality"—*Sewanee Review*, Volume 55, July, 1947, pp. 357-83. (Reprinted in *A Southern Vanguard: The John Peale Bishop Memorial Volume*, Allen Tate, ed., New York: Prentice Hall, 1947, pp. 100-121.)

"Time, Life and Fortune" — *View Magazine*, Spring, 1947, pp. 33-37.

"Henry IV, a Mirror for Magistrates" — *University of Toronto Quarterly*, Volume 17, January, 1948, pp. 152-60.

"On Herbert's Virtue" — *Readings for Liberal Education*, L. G. Locke, W. M. Gibson and G. Arms, eds., 1948, pp. 534-5. (op. cit. 1943)

"Color-bar" of BBC English" — *Canadian Forum*, Volume 29, April, 1949, pp. 9-10.

"Mr. Eliot's Historical Decorum" — *Renascence*, Volume 2, #1, Autumn, 1949, pp. 9-15.

"Pound's Critical Prose" in *Examination of Ezra Pound: A Collection of Essays*, Peter Russell ed., Norfolk, Conn. New Directions Book, 1950, pp. 165-71.

Book Review of *Essays in Criticism 1920-1948* by R. W. Stallman, *University of Toronto Quarterly*, January, 1950, pp. 211-12.

"T. S. Eliot" — *Renascence*, Volume 3, #1, Autumn, 1950, pp. 43-47.

"A Survey of Joyce Criticism" — *Renascence*, #4, Autumn, 1951, pp. 12-18.

"American Novel Through 50 Years: John Dos Passos" — *America*, Volume 85, #3, June, 1951, pp. 332-34.

"The Folklore of Industrial Man" — *Neurotica*, Volume 8, #3, Spring, 1951, pp. 3-20. (Abstracted from *The Mechanical Bride: A Folklore of Industrial Man* — noted below.)

*The Mechanical Bride: A Folklore of Industrial Man* — New York: Vanguard Press, 1951.
— London, Routledge & Kegan-Paul, 1967.
— reissued in hard cover by Vanguard Press, 1967.
— paperback by Beacon Press, 1967.
— Japan: *Kikai No Hanayome* — Translated by Isaka Manabu, Tokyo: Takeuchi Shoten, 1968.

"John Dos Passos: Technique vs. Sensibility"— *Fifty Years of the American Novel: A Christian Appraisal*, Charles Gardiner, ed., New York: Scribners, 1951. pp. 151-64.

"Poetry and Opinion: Examination of Ezra Pound and Letters of Pound"— *Renascence*, Volume 3, #2, Spring, 1951, pp. 200-202.

"Joyce, Aquinas, and the Poetical Process"— *Renascence*, Vol. 4, #1, 1951, pp. 3-11.

"Tennyson and Picturesque Poetry"— *Essays in Criticism*, Volume 1, #3, July, 1951, pp. 262-82.

**1952**   "Auden: An Introductory Essay"— *Renascence* #4, Spring, 1952, pp. 220-221.

"The Poetry of Ezra Pound"— *Renascence* #2, Spring, 1952, pp. 215-217.

"Advertising as a Magical Institution"— *Commerce Journal*, (University of Toronto Commerce Club) January, 1952, pp. 25-29.

"The Aesthetic Moment in Landscape Poetry"— *English Institute Essays, 1951*, Alan Downe, ed., New York: Columbia University Press, 1952, pp. 168-81.

"Baseball Is Culture"— *CBC Times*, October 25, November 1, and November 8, 1952. (Publication of Professor McLuhan's talk on a *CBC Wednesday Night* show.)

"Word Index to James Joyce's *Ulysses*"— *Renascence*, Vol. 4, #2, Spring, 1952, pp. 186-87.

"Defrosting Canadian Culture"— *American Mercury*, Volume 74, #339, March, 1952, pp. 91-97.

"Technology and Political Change"— *International Journal*, Volume 7, Summer, 1952, pp. 189-95.

**1953**   "Light on a Dark Horse"— *Renascence* #5, Spring, 1953, pp. 157-159.

"From Eliot to Seneca" — a Review of George Williamson's *The Senecan Amble: A Study in Prose from Bacon to Collier*, in *University of Toronto Quarterly*, January, 1953, pp. 199-202.

"The Age of Advertising" — *Commonweal*, Volume 58, #23, September 11, 1953, pp. 555-57.

"Comics and Culture" — *Saturday Night*, Volume 68, #1, February 28, 1953, pp. 19-20.

"Culture Without Literacy" — *Explorations*, Volume 1 University of Toronto Press, December, 1953, pp. 117-27.

"James Joyce: Trivial and Quadrivial" — *Thought*, Volume 28, #108, Spring, 1953, pp. 75-98.

"The Later Innis" — *Queen's Quarterly*, Volume 60, #3, Autumn, 1953, pp. 385-94.

"Maritain on Art" — *Renascence*, Volume 6, Autumn, 1953, pp. 40-44.

"The Poetry of George Herbert and Symbolist Communication" — *Thought*, Autumn, 1953.

"Wyndham Lewis: His Theory of Art and Communication" — *Shenandoah*, Volume 4, Nos. 2-3, Autumn, 1953, pp. 77-88.

54 "Catholic Humanism and Modern Letters" — *Christian Humanism in Letters: The McAuley Lectures, Series 2, 1954*, St. Joseph College, West Hartford, Connecticut. 1954. pp. 49-67.

"Comics and Culture" — *Our Sense of Identity: A Book of Canadian Essays*, Malcolm Ross, ed., Toronto: Ryerson Press, 1954, pp. 240-46. Op. cit. 1953.

"Joyce, Mallarme and the Press" — *Sewanee Review*, Volume 62, #1, Winter, 1954, pp. 38-55.

"Media as Art Forms" — *Explorations*, Volume 3, August, 1954, University of Toronto Press, pp. 6-13.

"New Media as Political Forms" — *Explorations*, Volume 3, University of Toronto Press, August, 1954, pp. 120-6.

"Henley's Invictus" — *The Creative Reader: An Anthology of Fiction, Drama, and Poetry* by R. W. Stallman, R. E. Waters, eds. New York: Ronald Press, 1954. pp. 874-5. (Op. cit. 1944)

"Poetry and Society" — *Poetry*, Volume 84, #2, May, 1954, pp. 93-4.

"Sight, Sound and the Fury" — *Commonweal*, Volume 60, April 9, 1954, pp. 168-97.

"Through Emerald Eyes" — *Renascence* #6, Spring, 1954. pp. 157-158.

*Counterblast* — University of Toronto Press, 1954. (unpaged, side-stapled, 9 leaves, blue paper cover)

1955    "An Historical Approach to Media" — *Teachers College Record*, Volume 57, #2, November, 1955, pp. 104-110.

"Five Sovereign Fingers Taxed the Breath" — *Shenandoah*, Volume 7, #1, Autumn, 1955, pp. 50-52.

"Nihilism Exposed" — *Renascence* #8, Winter, 1955, pp. 97-99.

"Paganism on Tip-Toe" — *Renascence* #3, Spring, 1955, p. 158.

"Psychopathology of *"Time"* and *"Life"* — in *Scene Before You: A New Approach to American Culture* by Chandler Brossard, New York: Rinehart, 1955, pp. 147-60.

"Radio and Television vs. the ABCED-Minded" — *Explorations*, Volume 5, University of Toronto Press, June, 1955, pp. 12-18.

"The Poetry of T. S. Eliot" — *Renascence*, Vol. 3, #3, Spring, 1955.

"Space, Time and Poetry" — *Explorations*, Vol. 4, February 1955, University of Toronto Press, pp. 56-62.

"Wyndham Lewis" — *Renascence*, Vol. 7, #2, Winter, 1955.

**1956**   *Selected Poetry of Tennyson* — Marshall McLuhan, ed., Rinehart, New York, 1956.

"Educational Effects of Mass Media of Communications" — *The Teachers College Record*, Vol. 57, #6, March, 1956, pp. 400-403.

"The Media Fit the Battle of Jericho" — *Explorations*, Vol. 6, July, 1956, University of Toronto Press, pp. 15-19.

"Mimesis" — *Renascence*, Vol. 9, #2, Winter, 1956. (A Review of Trask's *Mimesis*)

"The New Languages" — *The Chicago Review*, Vol. 10, #1, Spring, 1956, pp. 46-52.

**1957**   "American Advertising" — *Mass Culture: The Popular Arts in America*, Bernard Rosenburg and David Manning White, eds., Glencoe, Illinois Free Press, 1957, pp. 435-42. (Op. Cit. 1947)

"Classrooms Without Walls" — *Explorations*, Vol. 7, March, 1957, University of Toronto Press, pp. 22-26.

"Coleridge as Artist" — *The Major English Romantic Poets: A Symposium in Reappraisal*, Clarence D. Thorpe, Carlos Baker, Bennet Weaver, eds., Southern Illinois University Press, Carbondale, Illinois, 1957, pp. 83-99.

"David Riesman and the Avant-Garde" — *Explorations*, Vol. 7, March, 1957, University of Toronto Press, pp. 112-16.

"The Effect of the Printed Book on Language in the Sixteenth Century — *Explorations*, Vol. 7, March, 1957, pp. 99-108.

"Jazz and Modern Letters"—*Explorations*, Vol. 7, March, 1957, pp. 74-76.

"Sight, Sound and the Fury"—*Mass Culture: The Popular Arts in America*, by Bernard Rosenburg and David Manning White, eds., Free Press, Glencoe, Illinois, 1957, pp. 489-95.

"Subliminal Projection on Project"—*Canadian Forum*, Vol. 37, December, 1957, pp. 196-97.

"Classroom T.V."—*Study Pamphlets in Canadian Education*, No. 12 (Toronto: Copp Clark, 1957), 8 pp.

"Why the CBC Must Be Dull"—*Saturday Night*, Vol. 72, February 16, 1957.

"The Third Program in the Human Age"—*Explorations*, Vol. 8 (Oct. 1957)

"Brain Storming"

"American Model, 1795"

"Electronics as ESP"

"The Be-Spoke Tailor"

"The Journalist's Dilemma"

"The Pattern of Oral Strategy in the USSR"

"The Bathroom Baritone and the Wide-Open Spaces"

"Stress"

"Oral-Anal"

"Sherlock Holmes vs. the Bureaucrats"

"Verbi-Voco-Visual"

"Print as Patterkiller"

"Milton Had His Daughters, I Have My Dictaphone"

"The Alchemy of Social Change"

"The Organization Man"

"Characterization in Western Art, 1600-1900"

"The Liturgical Review"

"Television Murders Telephony"

"Picture of the World"

"Churchill Mobilizes the English Language"

"Eminent Extrapolators"

"The Old New Rich and the New New Rich"

"No Upside Down in Eskimo"

_____, *Explorations*, Vol. 8, October, 1957.

**)58** "Classic Treatment" — *Renascence* #10, Winter, 1958, pp. 102-103.

"Compliment Accepted" — *Renascence* #10, Winter, 1958, pp. 106-108.

"Media Alchemy in Art and Society" — *The Journal of Communication*, Volume 8, #2, Summer, 1958, pp. 63-67.

"Eliot's Poetry and Plays" — *Renascence*, Vol. 10, #2, Winter, 1958.

"The Electronic Revolution in North America" — *International Literary Annual No. 1*, John Wain, ed., London: John Calder, 1958, pp. 165-69.

"Knowledge, Ideas, Information and Communication" — *Yearbook of Education*, 1958, pp. 225-32.

"One Wheel, All Square" — *Renascence*, Vol. 10, #4, Summer, 1958.

Untitled speech with question and answer period added, in *Radio: In the Culture of Canada*. A national conference sponsored by the British Columbia Association of Broadcasters and the University of British Columbia, Vancouver, B.C., May 5-9, 1958. Article pp. 4-9, questions and answers pp. 9-14.

"Our New Electronic Culture" — *NAEB Journal*, Vol. 18, #1, October, 1958, pp. 19-20 and 24-26.

"Culture Is Our Business" — *NAEB Journal*, Vol. 18, #2, December, 1958, pp. 1-5 and 30-34.

"Communications and Education" — *The Basilian Teacher*, Vol. 2, #6, March, 1958, pp. 11-16.

1959    "The Letters of William Butler Yeats" — *Renascence*, Vol. 11, #3, Spring, 1959.

"On Poetry and Poets" — *Renascence*, Vol. 11, #2, Winter, 1959.

"Analysts' Statement" — *Current Issues in Higher Education*, 1959, pp. 176-81. (G. Kerry Smith, ed., Washington, D.C. Association for Higher Education.)

"Joyce or No Joyce" — a Review of *Joyce Among the Jesuits* in *Renascence*, Vol. 12, #1, Autumn, 1959, pp. 53-54.

"Myth and Mass Media" — *Daedalus*, Vol. 88, #2, Spring, 1959, pp. 339-48.

"Printing and Social Change" — *Printing Progress: A Mid-Century Report* by The International Association of Printing House Craftsmen Inc., Cincinnati, 1959, pp. 81-112.

"Communication Media — Makers of the Modern Mind" — *Communications* — published by St. Michael's College, University of Toronto, re Annual Seminarians' Conference August 29-31, 1959, pp. 9-22.

"Virgil, Yeats, and 13000 Friends" — *Renascence*, #11, Winter, 1959, pp. 94-95.

"Acoustic Space"

"Classroom Without Walls" (op. cit. 1957)

"Five Sovereign Fingers Taxed the Breath" (op. cit. 1955)

"Media Log"

"The Effect of the Printed Book on Language in the 16th Century"

_____ all five articles in *Explorations in Communication,* Edmund Carpenter and Marshall McLuhan eds., Boston: Beacon Hill Press, 1960. (Published in Italy, 1966 — Spain, 1968 — Japan, 1968.)

"The Effects of the Improvement of Communication Media"—*Journal of Economic History,* Volume 20 (Dec. 1960), pp. 566-75.

"Electronics and the Changing Role of Print"—*Audio-Visual Communication Review (The Education of the AV Communication Specialist,* the proceedings of a DAVI seminar, Fred Harcleroad ed.), Volume 8, #5, Sept./Oct. 1960, pp. 74-83.

"A Critical Discipline"—*review* of *A Portrait of the Artist as the Enemy,* Wyndham Lewis—*Renascence,* Vol. 12, #2, Winter, 1960, pp. 93-95.

"Another Eliot Party"—*review* of *T. S. Eliot: A Symposium for his 70th Birthday,* by N. Braybrooke, *Renascence,* Vol. 12, #3, Spring, 1960, pp. 156-57.

"Around the World, Around the Clock"—*review* of *The Image Industries* by Wm. Lynch, in *Renascence,* Vol. 12, #4, Summer, 1960, pp. 204-5.

"Romanticism Reviewed"—*review* of *Romantic Image* by Frank Kermode, *Renascence,* Vol. 12, #4, Summer, 1960, pp. 207-9.

"Flirting with Shadows"—*review* of *The Invisible Poet: T. S. Eliot,* by Hugh Kenner, in *Renascence,* Vol. 12, #4, Summer, 1960, pp. 212-14.

"The Personal Approach"—*review* of *Shakespeare and Co.*, by Sylvia Beach, *Renascence*, Volume 13. #1, Autumn, 1960, pp. 42-43.

*Report on Project in Understanding New Media* prepared for and published by The National Association of Educational Broadcasters for the Department of Education, Washington, D.C., 1960. (137 pp.)

"Grammar for the Newer Media"—*Communication in General Education*, edited by Shoemaker-Forsdale. Published by Wm. C. Brown Company, Dubuque, Iowa, 1960, pp. 17-27.

"Joyce as Critic"—*Renascence* #12, Summer, 1960, pp. 202-3.

"Myth, Oral, and Written"—*Commentary*, #29, July, 1960, pp. 90-91.

"Melodic and Scribal"—*review* of *Song in the Works of J. Joyce*, by M. J. C. Hodgart & M. P. Worthington, *Renascence*, Volume 13, #1, Autumn, 1960, page 51.

"The Medium is the Message"—*Forum* (Houston), Spring, 1960, pp. 19-24.

"Myth and Mass Media"—*Myth and Mythmaking*, Henry A. Murray ed., New York: Braziller, 1960, pp. 288-99. (op. cit. 1959)

"New Media and the New Education"—*Christianity and Culture*, J. S. Murphy ed., Helicon, 1960, pp. 181-90. (Also appeared under title "Electronics and the Changing Role of Print," op. cit. 1960.)

"Tennyson and Picturesque Poetry"—*Critical Essays on the Poetry of Tennyson*, by John Kilham ed., London: Routledge and Kegan Paul, 1960, pp. 67-85. (op. cit. 1951)

"Tennyson and the Romantic Epic"—*Critical Essays on the Poetry of Tennyson*, cited above, pp. 86-95.

1961   "James Joyce"—*Renascence*, Volume 13, #4, Summer, 1961.

"The Books at the Wake" — *Renascence*, Volume 13, #4, Summer, 1961.

"The Humanities in the Electronic Age" — *Humanities Association Bulletin* (Canada), Volume 34, #1, Fall, 1961, pp. 3-11. Also appeared in *Thought From the Learned Societies of Canada*, Toronto: W. J. Gage, 1961, pp. 5-14.

"Inside the Five Sense Sensorium" — *Canadian Architect*, Volume 6, #6, June, 1961, pp. 49-54.

"New Media and the New Education" — *The Basilian Teacher*, Volume 6, #3, December, 1961, pp. 93-100. (op. cit. 1960)

"Producers and Consumers" — *Renascence* #13, Summer, 1961, pp. 217-219.

**962**  "Review of Jacques Maritain's *Art and Scholasticism*" — *Dalhousie Review* #42 (Winter 1962/63), p. 532.

"A Fresh Perspective on Dialogue" — *The Superior Student*, Volume 4, Jan./Feb. 1962, pp. 2-6.

"Joyce, Aquinas and the Poetic Process" in *Joyce's Portrait: Criticisms and Techniques*, Thomas E. Connolly ed., New York: Appleton-Century-Crofts, 1962, pp. 249-65. (op. cit. 1951)

"The Electronic Age — The Age of Implosion" in *Mass Media in Canada*, John A. Irving ed., Toronto: Ryerson Press, 1962, pp. 179-205.

"Prospect" — *Canadian Art*, Volume 19, Sept./Oct. 1962, pp. 363-66.

*The Gutenberg Galaxy: The Making of Typographic Man*, Marshall McLuhan. Toronto: University of Toronto Press, 1962, 293 pages. Paperback edition in Canadian University Paperbacks series by the same publisher. (Also published in Germany, 1968 — Stockholm, 1969 — Japan, 1968 — Montreal, 1967 — Spain, 1969 — etc. — twenty-two translations in all.)

"Two Aspects of the Communications Revaluation" — *Canadian Communications*, Volume 2, #2.

"Prospect of America" — *University of Toronto Quarterly*, Volume 32, #1, October, 1962, pp. 107-8.

"The Chaplin Bloom" — *Renascence* #14, Summer, 1962, pp. 216-17.

"Phase Two" — *Renascence* #14, Summer, 1962, pp. 166-167.

1963     "We Need a New Picture of Knowledge" in *New Insights and the Curriculum Development*, Washington: National Education Association, 1963, pp. 57-70.

"The Agenbite of Outwit" — *Location*, Volume 1, #1, Spring, 1963.

"Another Eliot Party" — *Renascence* #12, Spring, 1963, p. 156.

1964     "Printing and the Mind" — *Times Literary Supplement*, London, England, June 19, 1964, pp. 517-18.

"Pop Art Avant Garde?" — *AV Communications Review*, #12, Spring, 1964, pp. 217-18.

"Murder by Television" — *The Canadian Forum*, Volume 43, #516, January, 1964, pp. 222-23.

"John Dos Passos: Technique vs. Sensibility" — *Modern American Fiction: Essays in Criticism*, Litz A. Walton, ed., Oxford: Galaxy Book, 1964, pp. 138-49. (op. cit. 1951)

"Masks and Roles and the Corporate Society" — *Varsity Graduate*, Volume 11, #2, Summer, 1964, pp. 61-64.

*Forward* to "Vision and Reading Achievement" by W. A. Hurst, in *Canadian Journal of Optometry*, Volume 25, #4, April, 1964, pp. 3-5.

"Decline of the Visual" — *Dot Zero* (published by the National Society of Art Directors, New York), May, 1964.

*Understanding Media* — Marshall McLuhan. New York: McGraw-Hill Publishing Company, May, 1964. Paperback edition by same publisher, Spring, 1965. Signet paperback edition, November, 1966.
Published in Italy, 1967 — Norway, 1968 — Denmark, 1967 — Sweden, 1967 — England, 1967 — Germany, 1968 — Japan, 1968 — Finland, 1968 — Spain, 1968 — France, 1968 — Mexico, 1969 — Sao Paulo, 1969 — Montreal, 1968 — Utrecht, 1969 —

"Radio: The Tribal Drum" — *AV Communication Review*, Vol. 12, #2, pp. 133-45.

"New Media and the Arts" — *Arts in Society*, University of Wisconsin Press, Volume 3, #2, September, 1964.

"The University in the Electric Age: The End of the Gap Between Theory and Practice" — *Varsity Graduate*, University of Toronto Press, Volume 11, #3, December, 1964, pp. 60-64.

"Notes on Burroughs" — a *review* of *The Naked Lunch* and *Nova Express* by Wm. Burroughs — *Nation*, December, 1964, pp. 517-19.

*Preface* for reprinting of *The Bias of Communication*, by H. A. Innis. Toronto: University of Toronto Press, Fall, 1964.

ɔk  *Voices of Literature, Volume 1* — an anthology of verse in two volumes by Marshall McLuhan and Richard Schoeck, New York: Holt, Rinehart and Winston, 1964, 247 pages.

"Culture and Technology" — *Times Literary Supplement*, London, England, #3258, August 6, 1964.

65  *Voices of Literature, Volume II* — Marshall McLuhan and Richard Schoeck, New York: Holt, Rinehart and Winston, 1965. 247 pages.

*Preface* for the paperback edition of *Understanding Media*, New York: McGraw-Hill, Spring, 1965.

"Art as Anti-Environment" — *Art News Annual*, New York, Volume 31, February, 1965.

"A New Journey for the Magi" — *Decisive Years,* Toronto: Baker Publishing Company, April, 1965, pp. 12-16.

"The Relation of Environment to Anti-Environment" — *Communication: The Human Dialogue,* by Floyd Matson and Ashley Montagu. Glencoe, Illinois Free Press, 1965.

"Guaranteed Income in the Electric Age, Part III, "The Social View" in *The Guaranteed Income: A Symposium in Income Distribution in a Cybernated Era* — Robert Theobald, New York: Doubleday Publication, Fall, 1965.

*Review* of *A Dictionary of Modern English Usage* by H. W. Fowler, second edition revised by Sir Ernest Gowers (Oxford: Clarendon Press, 1965) in *Saturday Night* magazine.

*Review* of *Propaganda: The Formation of Men's Attitudes* by Jacques Ellul (New York: Alfred A. Knopf, October, 1965) in *New York Herald Tribune: Book Week.*

"The Emperor's Old Clothes" — *Vision + Value Series,* Gyorgy Kepes, ed., under title "The Man-Made Object," New York: George Braziller Inc., 1966, pp. 90-95.

"T. S. Eliot" — *The Canadian Forum,* Vol. XLIV, #529, February, 1965, pp. 243-44. (Transcript of talk by Prof. McLuhan given on CBC "Critically Speaking" program of January 10, 1965.)

"Big Transistor is Watching You" — *New York Herald Tribune Book Section,* November 28, 1965, p. 5.

*Review* of *Cyborg: Evolution of the Superman,* by D. S. Halacy, Jr., (New York: Harper and Row, 1965) — *Winnipeg Free Press.*

*Review* of *Alice's Adventures Under Ground* by Lewis Carroll, *New York Herald Tribune: Book Week,* October, 1965.

*Remarks* in *Technology in Learning,* Ontario Curriculum Institute: an interim report of the Study Committee on Institutional Aids and Techniques, May, 1965, pp. 32-39.

*Patterns of Literary Criticism* — General Editors: Marshall McLuhan, R. J. Schoeck, Ernest Sirluck. University of Chicago Press, 1965-71. Series — Volumes 1 to 10.

66 *Address at Vision '65* — transcript of talk given by Professor McLuhan at the University of Southern Illinois on October 23, 1965, which appeared in *The American Scholar,* Spring, 1966, pp. 196-205.
... retitled "Environmental Change and the New Technology," *Dicta* magazine, #8, October, 1966, p. 18.
... retitled "The Invisible Environment" in *Perspecta* (The Yale Architectural Journal), #11, Fall, 1966.
... retitled "The All-at-once World of Marshall McLuhan" in *British Vogue,* April, 1966.
... retitled "Technology and Environment" in *arts/canada* #105, February, 1967, pp. 5-7.
... retitled "Our Dawning Electric Age" in *Technology and Social Change* by Emmanuel Mesthene, New York: Bobbs-Merrill Company Inc., 1967.
... retitled "Great Changeovers For You" in *Vogue* #148, July, 1966, pp. 62-3.

"The Analogical Mirrors" in *Hopkins,* G. H. Hartman ed., April, 1966. (op. cit. 1945)

"The Crack in the Rear-View Mirror" — *McGill Journal of Education,* Spring, 1966, pp. 31-34.

*Review* of *Communication and Language* by Sir Gerald Barry, Dr. J. Bronowski, James Fisher and Sir Julian Huxley (London: Macdonald & Company, 1965) — *Times Literary Supplement,* February, 1966. (London, England)

"An Interview with Marshall McLuhan" — taped talk with Eli Bornstein, editor of *The Structuralist* — Special issue on Art and Technology — #6, June, 1966, University of Saskatchewan.

"From Gutenberg to Batman" — transcript of talk given by Professor McLuhan at the Annenberg School of Communication, Pennsylvania, on April 28, 1966, in July issue of *Vogue* magazine, retitled "Great Changeovers For You."

"We and Us" — *The Listener* (London, England) #75, May 26, 1966, p. 748.

"From Instruction to Discovery" — *Media and Methods,* Volume 3, #2, October, 1966, pp. 8-11. — retitled "Electronics and the Psychic Drop-Out" in *This Magazine Is About Schools,* Vol. 1, #1, April, 1966.

"Questions and Answers with Marshall McLuhan" — *Take One,* Volume 1, #2, November, 1966, pp. 7-10.

"Culture and Technology" — *Astronauts of Inner Space: An International Collection of Avant-Garde Activity,* Jack Berner ed., San Francisco: Stolen Paper Review Editions, 1966.

"The Brave New World of Marshall McLuhan" — interview *Glamour,* Volume 55, #5, July, 1966, pp. 100-101 and 133-35.

"Television in a New Light" in *The Meaning of Commercial Television* — Stanley T. Donner, ed., University of Texas Press, 1966, pp. 87-107.

"Marshall McLuhan and Mike Wallace: A Dialogue" — The Diebold Research Program Dinner, September 13, 1966 in New York City (taped interview) in booklet *The Diebold Research Program* Document #PP10, pp. 1-21.

"Circuitry" — excerpt from talk given by Professor McLuhan to Airlie Foundation on April 1, 1966 at Warrenton, Virginia. Pamphlet issued by The Wemyss Foundation, Wilmington, Delaware.

"The Relation of Environment to Anti-Environment," *University of Windsor Review,* Volume 11, #1, Fall, 1966, pp. 1-10.

**67** "Marshall McLuhan Massages the Medium" — *Nations Schools*, Volume 79, #6, June, 1967, pp. 36-37.

"The Humanities in the Electric Age" — *The Book of Canadian Prose II*, Toronto: W. J. Gage, 1967, (op. cit. 1961)

"The Medium is the Message" — *NEA Journal* #56, October, 1967, pp. 24-27.

"Santa Claus Gets the Message" — *McCalls* #94, December, 1967, p. 97.

"Parts of a Talk" — *Television Quarterly* #6, Fall, 1967, pp. 39-44.

"The Future of Education" — Marshall McLuhan and George Leonard — *Look*, Volume 31, #15, February 21, 1967, pp. 23-25.

"What TV is Really Doing to your Child" — *Family Circle*, Volume 70, #3, March 1967, pp. 33 and 98-100.

"Love" — *Saturday Night*, Volume 82, #2, pp. 25-28, Feb. 1967.

"The New Education" — *The Basilian Teacher*, Volume 2, #2, pp. 66-73. Reprinted in *Catholic Mind*, Volume 65, May, 1967, pp. 11-16.

"Environment" — *To Everything There is a Season* by Roloff Beny, Toronto: Longmans, 1967, pp. 312-13.

"Information Hunt Looms Big" — *College and University Journal*, Volume 6, #2, Spring, 1967, pp. 3-7.

"Technology: Its Influence on the Character of World Trade and Investment" — Professor McLuhan's address to the U.S. Department of Commerce, National Bureau of Standards, Gaithersburg, Maryland, on November 16, 1966 appeared in *Technology and World Trade: Proceedings of a Symposium* — NBS Miscellaneous publication #284, Washington, D.C., U.S. Printing Office, 1967.

"A McLuhan Montage"—quotations from NBC-TV show, March 1967 "The Medium is the Massage," also Channel 13 WNDT Educational Broadcasting Corporation from the May 15, 1966 program called "McLuhan on McLuhanism" in *School Library Journal,* April, 1967, Volume 13, #8, pp. 39-41.

*Preface* and *Comments* in *McLuhan: Hot and Cool*—Gerald Stearn, ed., Dial Press, New York, 1967.

*Verbi-Voco-Visual Explorations*—Something Else Press, New York, N.Y. 1967. Reprint of *Explorations 8.*

"Understanding Canada and Sundry Other Matters," *Mademoiselle,* Volume 64, #3, January, 1967 (taped interview).

"The Future of Sex"—Marshall McLuhan and George Leonard—*Look*—Volume 31, #15, pp. 56-63, July 25, 1967.

"The Future of Morality: The Inner vs. the Outer Quest," *The New Morality,* Wm. Dunphy, ed. New York: Herder and Herder, 1967, pp. 175-189.

"Money: The Poor Man's Credit Card" (excerpt from *Understanding Media*) in *Stewardship Facts 1967-68* (booklet published annually for ministers and church leaders by the National Council of the Churches of Christ, New York, N.Y.), pp. 48-59.

*The Medium Is The Massage*—Marshall McLuhan and Quentin Fiore, Bantam paperback, N.Y. and Toronto, 1967.
— published in hard cover, 1967.
— published in England by Penguins, 1967 — France, 1968 — Germany, 1969 — Buenos Aires, 1969 — Italy, 1968 — Japan, 1968.

"Toronto Is a Happening"—*Toronto Life,* September, 1967, Volume 1, #11, pp. 23-29. (photography by Robert McCormick)—Photograph of Marshall McLuhan on cover.

"The Car As a Toy" — *Macleans,* Volume 80, #9, September, 1967, pp. 14. Photograph of Professor McLuhan on cover.

Transcript of talk which Professor McLuhan gave at Georgetown University Symposium in November, 1964, published in *The Social Impact of Cybernetics,* Charles R. Dechert, ed., 1967. (The volume consists of the papers presented at the Symposium.) Publisher: University of Notre Dame press.

"McLuhan on Education" — *The Argus,* Lakehead University Newspaper, Vol. 2, #111, October 5, 1967, p. 6-7. (Also appeared in *Catholic Trustee,* Vol. 7, #4, December, 1967 — retitled "Marshall McLuhan," pp. 23-25.)

Address at Management Programming Seminar, New York, September 28, 1967 published by TV Stations Inc. in booklet *The Arts of Success,* March, 1968, pp. 51-57.

**968** "Environment as Programmed Happening" — *Knowledge and the Future of Man,* Walter Ong, ed., Publisher: Holt, Rinehart & Winston, 1968, pp. 113-124.

Excerpt from *Understanding Media* in *The Cool Medium: History of Popular Culture* by Norman Cantor and M. S. Werthman, eds., New York; Macmillan, 1968. pp. 718-726.

"McLuhan on Marketing" — remarks of Marshall McLuhan on marketing compiled by Anthony Liversidge in *VIP* magazine, Spring, #17, 1968, p. 35.

*War and Peace in the Global Village* — Marshall McLuhan and Quentin Fiore, New York: McGraw-Hill, 1968. Bantam paperback.

*Through the Vanishing Point: Space in Poetry and Painting* — Marshall McLuhan and Harley Parker, New York: Harper & Row, 1968.

Forward by Marshall McLuhan to "Response to New Media" in *Explorations* section of *The Graduate,* University of Toronto, Volume 11, #1, December, 1968, pp. 67-68.

"The Reversal of the Overheated Image"—*Playboy*, Volume 15, #12, December, 1968, pp. 131-134 and 245. (Interviewed by Eric Norden)

"All of the Candidates Are Asleep"—*The Saturday Evening Post*, August, 1968, #16, pp. 34-36.

*Preface* to *Simplified Cybernetics: The Feedback Story* by Arthur Porter, English University Press, 1969.

*Preface* to *Time: The Fourth Dimension of the Mind* by Dr. Robert Wallis, New York: Harcourt Brace and World, 1968.

"Adopt a College"—*This Magazine is About Schools*, Volume 2, #4, Autumn, 1968, pp. 50-55.

"Fashion Is The Medium"—*Harpers Bazaar*, #101, April, 1968, pp. 123-150.

"Fashion Is Language: McLuhan's Bazaar"—*Harpers Bazaar*, #101, April, 1968, pp. 150-167.

"Guaranteed Income in the Electric Age"—*Beyond Left and Right*—Richard Kostelanetz, ed., Apollo paperback A-202, Wm. Morrow & Company, New York, 1968, pp. 72-83. (op. cit. 1965)

*Review* of *Federalism and the French Canadians* by Pierre E. Trudeau, New York: St. Martin's Press, 1968. *New York Times Book Review*, October 28, 1968.

*Review* of *The Revolution of Hope* by Erich Fromm, "World Perspectives," Volume 38, Harper and Row, New York, 1968. *Book World*, New York, October 9, 1968.

*McLuhan Dew-Line Newsletters*—published by The Human Development Corporation, 119 Fifth Avenue, New York, N.Y.:

"Black Is Not a Color"—#1, July, 1968.

"When You Call Me That, Smile!" #2, August, 1968."

"A Second Way to Read War and Peace in the Global Village," #3, September, 1968.

"McLuhan Futuregram" #1:
                                    (Big
Culture Is Our (New Business — #4, October, 1968
                                    (Hot

"Through the Vanishing Point" — #5, November, 1968.

"Communism: Hard and Soft" — #6, December, 1968.

\*\*\*\*\*\*\*\*\*\*\*\*

"Is the Book Dead?" — *Clearing House* #17, March, 1968, pp. 447-8.

**1969**  *Counterblast* — Marshall McLuhan and Harley Parker, New York: Harcourt-Brace, 1969. (London, England: Rapp & Whiting — Canada: McClelland and Stewart Ltd.)

*Review* of *Time Inc.* by Robert T. Elson, ed., New York: Atheneum Publishers, 1968, in International Journal, Toronto, March 29, 1969.

Contributions to *Spectrum of Catholic Attitudes* — Milwaukee: Bruce Publishing — pp. 93-4, 124-5, 130-32, 138-9, 146-7, 159-60, 167-8.

"Media and the Making of the Mid-West" — *Chicagoland,* July, 1969, Volume 6, #9, pp. 11-16.

"Retribalized Makers" — *Natural Enemies??* — Alexander Klein, ed., Philadelphia and New York: J. B. Lippincott Company, pp. 341-346.

"Learning in the Global Village" — *Radical School Reform,* Ronald and Beatrice Gross, ed., Simon & Schuster, New York, 1969, pp. 106-115. (Reprint of "The Future of Education" by Marshall McLuhan and George Leonard, op. cit. 1967.)

*The Hardware/Software Mergers: Hot Successful Have They Been?* Panel discussion: Marshall McLuhan, Francis Keppel, Ralph W. Tyler, Harold Haizlip and Jonathan Kozol — Proceedings of a conference held November 16, 1969, at the Center for Continuing Education, University of Chicago, sponsored by Urban Research Corporation who published paper.

"Preliminary Observations on Breakdown as Breakthrough," University of Toronto *Graduate*, Volume 11, #2, pp. 82-85, March, 1969.

"Harold Innis" — University of Toronto *Graduate*, Volume 11, #3, June, 1969, pp. 91-99.

*Mutations 1990* — Book of selected essays by Marshall McLuhan published by Maison Mame, France. The book includes "What TV Is Really Doing to Your Children" — "Great Changeovers For You" — "The Future of Education" — "The Future of Sex." (Published by Editions HMH, Montreal, 1969 — Holland, 1970)

*The Interior Landscape: Selected Literary Criticism* — Marshall McLuhan, edited by Eugene McNamara, New York: McGraw-Hill, 1969. Published by Claasen Verlag GmbH, Dusseldorf, Germany, 1974.

Excerpts from *Counterblast* appeared in Toronto Star together with artist's sketch of Marshall McLuhan on Friday, November 21, 1969. Second excerpt — November 28. Third excerpt, December 5, 1969.

"Wyndham Lewis" — *Atlantic Monthly,* December, 1969, Volume 224, #6, pp. 93-98.

"Communication in the Global Village" — *This Cybernetic Age,* by Don Toppin. New York: The Human Development Corporation, 1969, pp. 158-167.

*McLuhan Dew-Line Newsletters* — published by The Human Development Corporation, New York:

"Vertical Suburbs are Hi-Rise Slums" Volume 1, #7, January, 1969.

"The Mini-State and the Future of Organization," Volume 1, #8, February, 1969.

"Problems of Communicating with People Through Media" — Vol. 1, #9, March, 1969.

"Breakdown as Breakthrough" — Vol. 1, #10, April, 1969.

"Strike the Set" — Vol. 1, #11, May, 1969.

"Ad Verse: Ad Junet" — Vol. 1, #12, June, 1969.

"Media and the Structured Society" — Vol. 2, #1, July/August, 1969. (with card deck)

"Inflation as New Rim-Spin" — Vol. 2, #2, Sept./Oct. 1969.

"The End of Steel and/or Steal: Corporate Criminality vs. Collective Responsibility" — Vol. 2, #3, Nov./Dec. 1969.

"Playboy Interview: Marshall McLuhan" — *Playboy*, March, 1969. Interviewer Eric Norden. Vol. 16, #3, pp. 53-74 and 158.

"Ideas on the Church" — Professor McLuhan interviewed by Hubert Hoskins in *The Listener*, London, England, March 26, 1970.

"Where It's At" — *Campus Call*, Volume x, #5, January, 1970, pp. 3-4.

"Identity, Technology and War" — comments by Marshall McLuhan on "The Joys of War" by James Parker which had been published in *U.S. Catholic Jubilee*. This article appeared in *U.S. Catholic Jubilee*, Vol. XXXV, #1, 1970, pp. 36 and 37.

"McLuhan's Eye View" — *St. Michael's College Newsletter*, Vol. 8, #2, Spring, 1970.

*Introduction* to *The De-Romanization of the American Catholic Church* — Edward Wakin and Father Joseph F. Scheuer, New American Library, Plume Book, 1970, pp. xi to xiii.

"The University and the City" — University of Toronto *Graduate*, Vol. 111, #2, pp. 75-80, April, 1970.

"Classroom Without Walls" — *The American Experience: A Radical Reader* by Harold Jaffee and John Tytell, 1970, pp. 293-297. (op. cit. 1957)

"1959 — Electronic Revolution" — address delivered at the 1959 Conference of the American Association for Higher Education in Washington in *1945 Twenty Five Years 1970* — G. Kerry Smith ed., published by The American Association for Higher Education, 1970, pp. 96-104.

"The Motorcar: The Mechanical Bride" — *Confrontation: Psychology and the Problems of Today* — Dr. John Lyman, ed., Chicago, Ill.: Scott, Foresman & Company, 1970, pp. 319-322.

*Culture Is Our Business* — Marshall McLuhan — New York: McGraw-Hill, 1970.

*McLuhan Dew-Line Newsletters* — published by The Human Development Corporation, New York:

"Agnew Agonistes" — Vol. 2, #4, Jan./Feb. 1970.

"Bridges" — Vol. 2, #5, Mar./April, 1970.

"The Genuine Imitation Fake" — Vol. 2, #6, May/June, 1970.

"The City as University" — Vol. 2, #7, July/Aug. 1970.

"McLuhan on Religion" — *Christianity Today*, February 13, 1970, p. 34.

*Voices of Literature: Sounds, Masks, Roles,* Volume III, Marshall McLuhan and R. J. Schoeck. New York: Holt, Rinehart and Winston, 1970.

"The Cement Kimono for the Disposable City" — Letter to the Editor of the *Globe and Mail,* Toronto, commenting on an article by Robert Tennent entitled "Auto Alternatives" which had appeared earlier. March 14, 1970.

Letter to Mr. Tickton, Executive Director of the Commission on Instructional Technology appeared in *AV Communication Review*, Volume 18, #3, Fall, 1970, p. 307.

"Marshall McLuhan on the obsolescence of print" in Letters, Points of View Section, *Monday Morning*, May, 1970, Volume 4, #7.

*Editorial — Journal of Environmental Studies*, Volume 1, #1, October, 1970, p. 3 (London, England).

Letter to the Editor, *Globe and Mail*, Toronto, re Nicholas Cotter's report from Montreal on June 16th entitled "McLuhan Terms Press Obsolete" — June 17, 1970.

"War of the Icons" (Chapter 32 of *Understanding Media* plus two additional pages) in *Icons of Popular Culture* Marshall Fishwick and Ray Browne, eds., Bowling Green: Popular Culture Press, 1970.

*From Cliche to Archetype* — Marshall McLuhan and Wilfred Watson, New York: Viking Press, 1970.

"McLuhan on Russia: An Interview with Professor Gary Kern," *Abraxas*, No. 2, The University of Rochester, New York, Fall, 1970.

"Mini-Skirt Tribalism" — An Interview with Marshall McLuhan by Catherine Court — *Rags*, New York, October, 1970, p. 23. (Reprinted in *Twen* magazine, Germany, p. 82, December 12, 1970.)

"How TV and Radio Help the Cause of Groups Like the FLQ," *Toronto Star*, October 17, 1970, p. 7.

Professor McLuhan's reply to "Northrop Frye on Communications" in *The Listener*, London, England, October 8, 1970, Volume 84, #2167, pp. 475-6.

"Decentralization Takes Command" — *Toronto Star*, Saturday, October 17, 1970.

*Preface* for English publication of *Culture Is Our Business* — November 23, 1970.

"Discontinuity and Communication in Literature" —
*Problems of Textual Analysis*, P. R. Leon and P. Nes-
selroth, eds., Marcel Didier Canada Limited, Montreal,
1971. (Text of talk given at University College on November 21, 1970.)

"Cicero and the Renaissance Training for Prince and
Poet" — *Renaissance and Reformation*, Volume VI, #3,
CRRS, Victoria College, University of Toronto, pp. 38-42.

"The Ciceronian Program in Pulpit and in Literary Criticism" — *Renaissance and Reformation*, Volume VII,
#1, CRRS, Victoria College, University of Toronto, pp.
3-7.

"The Executive as Dropout" — Marshall McLuhan and
Barrington Nevitt in University of Toronto *Graduate*,
December, 1970, pp. 117-19.

"McLuhan Urges Book Critics to Search for Missing
Link," caption above Professor McLuhan's Letter to
the Editor of the *Toronto Star*, Saturday, December 19,
1970, p. 15.

"Education in the Electronic Age" — *Interexchange*,
Vol. 1, #4, 1970, pp. 1-12. (transcript of talk given to
Provincial Committee on Aims and Objectives of Education in the Schools of Ontario on January 19, 1967,
published by the Ontario Institute for Studies in Education.)

"The Man Who Came to Listen" — Marshall McLuhan
and Barrington Nevitt — *Peter Drucker's Contributions
to Business Enterprise*, Tony H. Bonaparte and J. E.
Flaherty eds., New York University Press, 1970, pp.
35-55.

Letter to the Editor — *The Listener*, London, England
in reply to Jonathan Miller's letter of July 15, 1971. Volume 86, #2213, August 26, 1971, pp. 272-273.

1971   An Interview with Marshall McLuhan — *The Mike*, St.
Michael's College, University of Toronto, Vol. XXII,
February 4, 1971, pp. 1-3.

*Letter* to the Editor of the *Toronto Star* re Peter Sypno-wich's review of McLUHAN by Jonathan Miller on February 25, 1971. Letter was published under the caption "McLuhan Critics of the World Unite" on March 16, 1971.

"Hijacking procedure of Cities" — Letter to the Editor of the *Toronto Star*, March 20, 1971.

The following articles appeared in the summer issue of the University of Toronto *Graduate*, Explorations Section, June, 1971, pp. 102-132:

> "Shakespeare, the Lay Rector of the Collegiate Church of the Holy Trinity, Stratford-upon-Avon"
>
> "Rock and the Sound of Music"
>
> "The Calley Trial and the Changing Patterns in the Judiciary"
>
> "The Hijacking of Cities, Nations, Planets in the Age of Spaceship Earth"
>
> "The Case of Eric Kierans and the Executive as Dropout"(Marshall McLuhan and Barrington Nevitt)

"Obiter dicta" — Letter in *Atlantic*, October, 1971, p. 38-40.

Marshall McLuhan Interviewed by Peter Newman — *Macleans* Magazine, Volume 84, #6, June, 1971, pp. 42 and 45.

"The Global Theatre" — *Ekistics*, Volume 32, #190, September, 1971, pp. 181-183. (Published by The Athens Centre of Ekistics, Athens, Greece.)

"McLuhan views the news: hot events on a cool medium where the audience is the actor" (Essay commissioned by ABC-TV Stations), *Television/Radio Age*, Vol. XIX, #3, September, 1971, pp. 32-33 and 71-72.

"Communication Needs Human Scale" — *Nursing Management*, Volume 1, #2, August, 1971, pp. 1-2. (Kendall Company of Canada Ltd. publication.)

"Polyanna Digest" — *Mass Media and the Popular Arts*, Frederic Rissover and David C. Birch, eds., 1971.

*Letter* to the Editor of *The Listener*, London, England, in reply to Jonathan Miller's letter of September 9, 1971. Appeared on October 28, 1971, Volume 86, #2222.

*Preface* to *Empire and Communications* by Harold Innis, University of Toronto Press re-printing, 1971.

"Erasmus: The Man and the Mask" — *Erasmus Newsletter*, University of Toronto Press, Volume 3, pp. 7-10.

*Preface* to *Training That Makes Sense* by A. J. Kirshner, Academic Therapy Publications, San Rafael, California, 1972, pp. 5-7.

Marshall McLuhan Interviewed by Gerard Moatti in *Les Informations*, No. 1376, September, 1971, pp. 88-93. (Paris, France)

"Classroom Without Walls" — *Perspectives on the Study of Film* — John Stuart Katz, Boston: Little, Brown and Company, 1971, pp. 22-24. Op. cit. 1957.

"On Russia: An Interview with Professor Gary Kern" — *International Education*, The University of Tennessee, Knoxville, Tennessee, Volume 1, #1, Fall, 1971, pp. 40-46. Op. cit. 1970.

Marshall McLuhan interviewed by Roger Mauge in *Paris Match*, No. 1176, November 20, 1971, pp. 14-26, Paris, France.

"Roles, Masks and Performances" — *New Literary History*, University of Charlottesville, Virginia, Volume 11, #3, Spring, 1971, pp. 517 to 531.

Under heading "How to Be as Well Informed As..." there is a short article by Professor McLuhan in *Macleans*, Vol. 84, #9, September, 1971.

Professor McLuhan quoted on pages 40, 125, 180 and 188 of *Dimensions of Change* by Don Fabun, Glencoe Press, Beverly Hills, California, 1971.

**972**   "The Yestermorrow of the Book" — *The UNESCO Courier* (published by UNESCO in thirteen languages), January, 1972, pp. 16, 17, 20.

An Interview with Professor McLuhan entitled "L'Express Va Plus Loin Avec Marshall McLuhan" — *L'Express*, February 20, 1972, #1075, Paris, France, pp. 68-74.

*Take Today: The Executive as Dropout* — Marshall McLuhan and Barrington Nevitt — New York: Harcourt, Brace, Jovanovich Inc., 1972. 304 pp.

Excerpt from *Take Today: The Executive as Dropout* — *MBA Magazine*, Volume 6, No. 7, April, 1972, pp. 16-18 and 56-59.

"Rocking the Liturgy" — *SMC Journal* (St. Michael's College Journal), Volume 1, #2, 1972, pp. 13-14.

"Everybody Into Nobody" — Marshall McLuhan and Barrington Nevitt — *New York Times*, page 3, July 16, 1972.

"Patterns Emerging in the New Politics" — *Globe and Mail*, Toronto, Friday, October 20, p. 7.

"Electric Age: Will the Worker be Left Behind?" — *Labour Gazette*, April, 1972, pp. 170-71.

"The Electric Age" — Letter to the Editor of the *Globe and Mail*, Toronto, September 21, 1972, p. 6.

"McLuhan Dissects the Executive" — Interview in *Business World*, June 24, 1972, p. 118.

"The Company We Keep — Trudeau and Nixon in the TV Vortex — Tarred with the same brush?" — *Saturday Night*, Toronto, December, 1972, p. 17.

"International Motley and Religious Costume" — *Christian Communication* (Saint Paul Society, Sherbrooke, P.Q.) December, 1972, Issue #39 — Newsletter.

**1973** "Do Americans Go to Church to be Alone?" — *The Critic* Volume XXXI, #3, Jan./Feb. 1973, pp. 14-23.

"Liturgy and Media" — *The Critic,* Volume XXXI, #4, Mar./April 1973, pp. 69-70. (Published by The Thomas More Association, Chicago, Illinois.)

"Cybernetics and Management" — Marshall McLuhan and Barrington Nevitt — *Kybernetes,* Volume 2, page 1. (Gordon & Breach Science Publishers Ltd., London, England), 1973.

"The Argument: Causality in the Electric World" — Marshall McLuhan and Barrington Nevitt — *Technology and Culture,* Vol. 14, #1, January, 1973, pp. 1-18. (University of Chicago Press)

*Letter* to the Editor of *The Listener,* London, England, re BBC Jubilee Edition — published January 4, 1973, Vol. 89, #2284, page 19.

"The Future of the Book" — in *Do Books Matter?,* published by Dunn and Wilson (Leeds) Ltd., London, England, 1973, pp. 31-41. (Published papers of seminar of The National Book League, 1973. President: HRH The Duke of Edinburgh.)

"Private Individual vs. Global Village" — chapter in *Abortion and Social Justice* by Thomas Hilgers and Dennis Horan. New York: Sheed and Ward, 1973, pp. 245-248.

*Preface* to *Subliminal Seduction* by Wilson Bryan Key, New Jersey: Prentice-Hall Inc., 1973.

"The Changing Nature of Communications" — *The Detroit News,* October 28, 1973, pp. 1E and 2E. (Part of series commemorating the 100th anniversary of the newspaper.)

"Mr. Nixon and the Dropout Strategy" — *The New York Times,* Sunday, July 29, 1973.

"The Printed Word: Architect of Nationalism" — *The Future of Literacy,* Robert Disch ed., 1973, pp. 34-48.

Profile and interview by Professor Derrick de Kerckhove in *Vie Des Arts*, pp. 19-23 (French) and 91-93 (English translation).

In the same issue there is an Editorial on Professor Mc-Luhan by Andree Paradis, p. 13 (English translation, p. 90). Same issue — article by Don Theall entitled "Les explorations esthetiques de McLuhan," pp. 14-18.

Volume XVIII, #72, Autumn, 1973, published by La Societe *La Vie Des Arts* — 360, rue McGill, Montreal, Canada.

"New Technology is Changing Human Identity" — *Toronto Star*, December 29, 1973, p. B-5.

"Television et Radiodiffusion," Marshall McLuhan and Derrick de Kerckhove in *Encyclopedia Universalis*, May 2, 1973 (published in Paris, France), pp. 894-898.

"Understanding McLuhan — and fie on any who don't" — *Globe and Mail*, Toronto, on Monday, September 10, 1973 on page 7 (full page with picture). Professor Mc-Luhan wrote this article in reply to an article by Richard Schickel entitled "Misunderstanding McLuhan" which appeared in the *Globe and Mail* on Friday, August 31, 1973.

"Watergate as Theatre" — *Performing Arts*, Volume X, #4, Winter, 1973, pp. 14-15. (Reprinted in *Indian Press* journal, Volume 1, #4, June, 1974, pp. 11-13, New Delhi, India.)

"Watergate — participatory torture, says McLuhan" — some excerpts from Professor McLuhan's address at York University's Osgoode Hall on October 17, 1973 — appeared in *Campus*, Volume 6, #3, pp. 3-4, November, 1973.

An interview with Marshall McLuhan by Jean Pare for *Forces* magazine, Number 22, 1973 (published by Hydro Quebec, Montreal), pp. 4-25. Many photos.

"The End of the Work Ethic" — an address to The Empire Club, Toronto, on November 16, 1972. Published by The Empire Club Foundation, 1973, in *The Empire Club Addresses 1972-73*, pp. 105-125.

1974 "Watergate as Theatre" — *Indian Press*, Volume 1, #4, June, 1974, pp. 11-13, New Delhi, India. Op. cit. 1973.

"At the moment of Sputnik the planet became a global theatre in which there are no spectators but only actors" — *Journal of Communications*, Volume 24:1, Winter, 1974, pp. 45-58. (Published by The Annenberg School, University of Pennsylvania.)

"An Intimate Look at Marshall McLuhan" — An Interview by Kaye Rowe — *The Brandon Sun* (Manitoba), February 2, 1974, p. 3.

Professor McLuhan's reply to the proposal by Kenneth Lamott in *Esquire* magazine that "Every American Should Get One Year Off in Every Seven" — page 68, February, 1974.

"Medium Meaning Message" — Marshall McLuhan and Barrington Nevitt in inaugural issue of *Communication* magazine, Vol. 1, #1, 1974, pp. 27-33 (published by Gordon & Breach Science Publishers Ltd., London, England)

"A Media Approach to Inflation" — *The New York Times*, September 21, 1974, p. L-29. (Marshall McLuhan and Barrington Nevitt)

"Mr. Eliot and the St. Louis Blues" — *The Antigonish Review*, #18, Summer, 1974, pp. 23-27 (published by St. Francis Xavier University, Antigonish, N.S.)

"A Discussion about Typewriters Between Marshall McLuhan, Some Poets and a Secretary" — by Jack Rose, also appeared in the above noted issue of *The Antigonish Review*, pp. 45-59.

*Letter* to the Editor of the *Toronto Star* regarding abortion appeared on the Editorial page, July 31, 1974.

"Learning a Living" — Chapter 10 in *The Future of Work*, Fred Best ed., Prentice-Hall Inc., Englewood Cliffs, N. J. 1974, pp. 103-113. ("Learning a Living" was editor's title — excerpt taken from *Understanding Media.*)

"Communication crisis in our global village: An Interview with Marshall McLuhan" — *Pegasus* (published annually by Mobil Oil Services Company Ltd., for worldwide Mobil group of companies). Interview by Gregory A. Vitiello, Editor, January, 1974, pp. 1-3.

"El camino a seguir en la investigacion de las comunicaciones" in *Dossier Mundo,* No. 32, April, 1974, pp. 6-8. An interview with Professor McLuhan done by Jose Luis Gomez (published by Ediciones Meridiano, S.A., Av. Infanta Carlota, 127, 8. A — Barcelona, Spain)

*Cliche a Archetype* — French version of *From Cliche to Archetype* published by Maison Mame in Paris, France, and HMH Hurtubise, Montreal, Quebec, 1974. (Completely re-written book, translation by Derrick de Kerckhove.)

"Eric and Marshall McLuhan — Gesetze der Medien — strukturelle Annaherung" — *Uterrichts Wissenschaft,* Beltz Verlag, Berlin, Germany, June, 1974, pp. 79-84.

An Interview with Marshall McLuhan by Jose Rague in *Teoria de la imagen* included in the series *Biblioteca Salvat de Grandes Temas.* Publisher: Salvat Editores, S.A., Barcelona, Spain, 1974.

"The Medieval Environment: Yesterday or Today?" — *Listening,* Volume 9, Nos. 1 and 2, Winter/Spring, 1974, pp. 9-27. University of Chicago Press.

"Making Contact with Marshall McLuhan" — an interview by Professor Louis Forsdale of Teachers College, Columbia University, New York, in *Electric Media,* published by Harcourt, Brace, Jovanovich Inc., N.Y. 1974, pp. 148-58.

"English Literature as Control Tower in Communication Study" — *The English Quarterly,* University of Waterloo, Volume 7, #1, Spring, 1974, pp. 3-7.

"McLuhan — McLuhan — McLuhan" — New York Times, May 10, 1974. (Reprinted in *Indian Press,* New Delhi, India, Volume 1, #5, July, 1974, pp. 11-12, retitled "Nixon and the Media.")

"X-Ray Vision" — short piece by Professor McLuhan in reply to an article entitled "What's in Store for Seventy-four?" — *Macleans,* Toronto, Volume 87, #1, p. 27, January, 1974.

*Introduction* to *Empedocles* by Helle Lambridis, published by University of Alabama Press, 1974.

"Liturgy and the Microphone"—*The Critic*, Volume XXXIII, #1, October/Nov./Dec. 1974, pp. 12-17.

"Francis Bacon: Ancient or Modern?"—*Renaissance and Reformation*, Volume X, 1974, #2, pp. 93-98. Published by Victoria College Centre for Renaissance and Reformation Studies, University of Toronto.

*Preface* to *Abortion in Perspective: The Rose Palace or the Fiery Dragon*—Donald DeMarco, published by Hiltz & Hayes Publishing Co. Ltd., Cincinnati, Ohio, 1974.

"The Future of Banking"—*Canadian National Bank (Montreal) 100th Annual Report Publication*, December, 1974, pp. x-xi.

**1975**   "The Medium is the Massage"—chapter in *Mass Media and Society*, Alan Wells, editor, published by Mayfield Publishing Company, Palo Alto, California, 1975, pp. 197-205.

"Communication: McLuhan's Laws of the Media" —*Technology and Culture*, Vol. 16, #1, January, 1975, pp. 74-78. (University of Chicago Press). Also published in *Indian Press*, Delhi, India, Vol. 11, #7, July, 1975, pp. 25-26.

*Letter* to the Editor of *James Joyce Quarterly*, Vol. 12, #3, Spring, 1975, p. 342. (re Ovid's *Metamorphoses* and *Dubliners*)

"The Changing Structures of Printing in the Electric Age"—*Humanities Association Review*, Vol. 26, #3, Summer, 1975, pp. 235 and 237. (Queen's University, Kingston, Ont.)

Guest columnist—*Today's Secretary*, New York, Vol. 78, #3, p. 4, December, 1975.

*Preface* to *You and Others: An Introduction to Interpersonal Communication* by Robert Soucie, Don MacRae, V. Gunckel, C. Hartleib and Ron Campbell. Toronto: McGraw-Hill Ryerson, 1975, pp. ix and x.

"At the Flip Point of Time: The Point of More Return?"
— *Communication Journal,* University of Pennsylvania,
Vol. 25, #4, Autumn, 1975, pp. 102-6.

"The Origins of Chesterton's Medievalism"— *The Chesterton Review,* Volume 1, #2, Spring /Summer, 1975,
pp. 49-50. (University of Saskatchewan, Saska-
toon, Sask.)

*Serialization* of *Take Today: The Executive as Dropout*
— Marshall McLuhan and Barrington Nevitt (Harcourt,
Brace, Jovanovich Inc., N.Y.— Canada: Longmans) op.
cit. 1972 in *Modern Office Procedures* (614 Superior
Avenue West, Cleveland, Ohio 44113) from February,
1975 to May, 1976.

"The Fourth World Demands Process Awareness,"
Volume 20, #2, February, 1975, pp. 16-20.

"Anticipating Progress," Volume 20, #3, March,
1975, pp. 14-18.

"The Executive as Artist," Volume 20, #4, April,
1975, pp. 14-18.

"Instant Information Makes Old Programs Obsolete," Volume 20, #5, May, 1975, pp. 14-18.

"Discovery Depends Upon Intuition and Surprise,"
Volume 20, #6, June, 1975, pp. 14-18.

"Innovations Require an Altered Perception," Volume 20, #7, July, 1975, pp. 14-18.

"Market Organization in the Information Age,"
Volume 20, #8, August, 1975, pp. 12-14 & 16.

"Obsolete Military Organization in Business,"
Volume 20, #9, September, 1975, pp. 18, 20 & 22.

"At Electric Speeds the effects of processes flip,"
Volume 20, #10, October, 1975, pp. 12-14 & 16.

"Executives must make history, not match past
errors," Volume 20, #11, November, 1975, pp. 20,
22 & 24.

"The Electronic World Affects Identity Images," Volume 20, #12, December, 1975, pp. 12-14 & 16.

1976

"New Patterns of Role Involvement," Volume 21, #1, January, 1976, pp. 16, 18 & 20.

"Information Speed-up Makes Involvement Mandatory," Volume 21, #2, February, 1976, pp. 16, 18 & 20.

"Answering Bureaucracy With Role Playing," Volume 21, #3, March, 1976, pp. 14-16.

"Efficiency Speed-up Destroys Effectiveness," Volume 21, #4, April, 1976, pp. 16-17.

"Extending Process Patterns to Their Effects," Vol. 21, #5, May, 1976, pp. 16, 18 & 20.

*Forward* to *The TV-Guided American* by Arthur Asa Berger, New York: Walker & Company, 1976, pp. vii-ix.

"Literature and the Scientific Knowledge of Man"— *Mosaic* No. D(S) 180, New Delhi, India, April, 1976, pp. 17-18 and 33.

"Formal Causality in Chesterton"— *The Chesterton Review*, Vol. 11, #2, Spring/Summer, 1976, pp. 253-259. (St. Thomas More College, University of Saskatchewan)

"The Violence of the Media"— *The Canadian Forum*, Vol. LVI, #664, September, 1976, pp. 9-12.

"La Violencia de los medios"— *Communicacion* magazine, #11-12, May/June, 1976, pp. 30-34. (Reprint of "The Violence of the Media"— Mexico)

"Misunderstanding the Media's Laws"— A Letter to the Editor, *Technology and Culture*, Vol. 17, #2, April, 1976, p. 263. (University of Chicago)

*Letter* to the Editor of the Toronto *Globe and Mail*— October 16, 1976 in reply to John Fraser's review of "Women of Trachis" staged at Hart House on October 7th. Mr. Fraser's review appeared in the *Globe and Mail* on October 8th entitled "Sophocles Tragedy Takes a Pounding."

Professor McLuhan's reply to the question: "What did you read when you were a child?" — *The Montreal Star*, Saturday, April 13, 1976, p. D-1. (with picture)

"Inside on the Outside, or the Spaced-Out American" —*Journal of Communication,* Autumn, 1976, Vol. 26, #4, pp. 46-53.

Quotations by McLuhan noted on pages 14, 121, 122, 172, 209, 216 and 108 of *Media Sexploitation* by Wilson Bryan Key, Prentice-Hall Inc., Englewood Cliffs, New Jersey, 1976.

"El norteamericano extravertido" — *Communicacion,* Ano 2, No. 14, August, 1976, pp. 17-21. (Publicacion Mensual de Comunicologia Aplicada de Mexico, S.A.)

Article about Wyndham Lewis in The Wyndham Lewis Society *Lewisletter* No. 5, Oct. 1976, p. 11. (Published in Glasgow, Scotland)

Letter to the Editor of the Toronto *Globe and Mail* re Blaik Kirby's review (December 6) of Arthur Hailey's *The Money Changers,* appeared December 11, 1976.

**1977**   "Futurechurch: Edward Wakin interviews Marshall McLuhan" — *U.S. Catholic,* Vol. 42, #1, January, 1977, pp. 6-7.

*Introduction* to *Faces of Canada* by George Lonn, Toronto: Pitt Publishing Co. Ltd., 1977. Article about Professor McLuhan on pages 39-41, picture on page 40.

*The City as Classroom* — Marshall McLuhan, Eric McLuhan and Kathy Hutchon. Toronto: The Book Society of Canada, 1977. (A Media Textbook for High Schools)

# Writings About Marshall McLuhan

**1944**   "Eliot's The Hippopotamus" by Francis Utley, *Explicator*, 3, November, 1944, no. 10.

**1951**   "March 22" - *Kirkus* #19 (February 1, 1951, p. 90.

"The Picture on Your Mind" - *Ammunition* (December, 1951).

**1952**   "Modern Folklore of Industrial Society" by Doris Boyle *Books on Trial*, #10 (April, 1952, p. 291).

"The Mechanical Bride" by Rudolph E. Morris, in *Renascence* 4, (Spring, 1952) p. 217. (Review of *Mechanical Bride*).

**1956**   "Editor's Note" by Lachlan MacDonald in *Chicago Review*, X (Spring, 1956) p. 52.

**1961**   "Multiple Provocation" by R.J. Baker, in *Canadian Literature*, #9, (Summer, 1961), p. 72. Review of *Explorations in Communications*.

**1962**   "Evils of Literacy" by A. Alverez in *New Statesman*, 64 (December 21, 1962) p. 902. Review of *Gutenberg Galaxy*.

"Books in General" - *Twentieth Century*, 157 (Winter, 1962-63) p. 168. Review of *Gutenberg Galaxy*.

*Review of Gutenberg Galaxy* by Stanley Donner in *Television Quarterly*, 1 (Nov. 1962) p. 74.

"Revolutions in Communications" by Tony Emery in *Canadian Literature* No. 13 (Autumn, 1962) p. 65. Review of *Gutenberg Galaxy*.

"The Gutenberg" by Geoffrey Gover in *Listener*, 68 (Dec. 8, 1962) p. 776. Review of *Gutenberg Galaxy*.

"Pilgrim of the Audile-Tactile" by John Simon, in *New Republic,* 147 (Oct. 8, 1962) p. 21. Review of *Gutenberg Galaxy.*

"The Gutenberg Galaxy" by Walter Ong, in *America,* 107 (Sept. 15, 1962) p. 743. Review of *Gutenberg Galaxy.*

*Revue de l'Universite de Ottawa,* 32 (Dec. 1962) p. 622.

*Worship,* 34 (Oct. 1962) p. 622

"Gutenberg and the Alphabet Blamed" - by Don Davin, *Globe & Mail,* Toronto, July 14, 1962, p. 16.

"Evils of Literacy" by A. Alverez in *New Statesman,* 64 (Dec. 21, 1962) p. 902. Review of *Gutenberg Galaxy.*

"Technology kills democracy McLuhan warns exchangers" - *The Varsity,* Vol. LXXXII, #26, Nov. 19, 1962.

"What did you say, Professor?" - article by Kildare Dobbs in *Star Weekly Magazine,* pp. 24-27, March, 1962.

"Civilization, human nature and the printing press" by John A. Irving, in *Canadian Saturday Night,* Oct. 1962. Review of *Gut. Galaxy.*

"Expect Violent Reaction to this Book" by Ronald Bates Review of *Gutenberg Galaxy - London Free Press,* October, 1962.

"Towards Electronic Man" - John Wain - Review of *Gutenberg Galaxy* in *The Observer Weekend Review,* Oct. 1962.

Review of *Gutenberg Galaxy* by John W. Mole - *Journalism Quarterly,* Autumn, 1962, p. 528.

"Print Changed the World, and McLuhan Tells How" by Tony Emery (Dept. of History, Victorial College) in *The Vancouver Sun,* Dec. 28, 1962.

"Toward an Understanding of Elect" by Lawrence Lipton in *Los Angeles Times,* December 30, 1962.

*The Letters of Wyndham Lewis* - W.K. Rose, ed., pub. by London, Methuen, 1962. Prof. McLuhan is involved in letters on pages 366-7-9, 370-2-3, 544-5, 554-5, 360-1, 376, 492, 500.

**1963**    "The Importance of Marshall McLuhan" by Arthur W. Foshay, *Educational Leadership,* Oct. 1963, p. 35.

"Are You a Linear and Sequential Thinker?" - AD from SUN (sent to office without date)

"The World of Marshall McLuhan" by John M. Culkin, Fordham University (check details)

Review of *Gutenberg Galaxy* in *Watauga Review,* published by Tennessee State University, Summer, 1963, pp. 23-25.

"Marshall McLuhan Wins Governor - General's Literary Award" in *Press Notes,* University of Toronto Press, Vol. 5, #4, Page 4. April, 1963.

*American Anthropologist,* #65 - article by Dell Hymes on page 478. April, 1963.

"Communication and Civilization" - by John K. Jessup in YALE REVIEW #52 (Spring, 1963) p. 454 - Rev. of *GG.*

"Between Two Galaxies" by Frank Kermode in ENCOUNTER, #20, (Feb. 1963), p. 76. Review of *GG.*

Review of *"The Gutenberg Galaxy"* by G.N. Leech in MODERN LANGUAGE REVIEW #58 (Oct. 1963), p. 542.

"Pilgrim of the Audile-Tactile" by John Simon in ACID TEST, 1963. Review of *GG.*

"Curvature of Typographic Man" by Paul Velde in JUBILEE, 11, (Aug. 1963) p. 42. Review of *GG.*

Review of *Gutenberg Galaxy* by R. Wiles in DALHOUSIE REVIEW, #43, Spring, 1963, p. 121.

Review of *The Gutenberg Galaxy* by Howard Winger in LIBRARY JOURNAL #33 (Oct. 1963) p. 352.

**'64** "The McLuhan Galaxy" by Kay Kritzwiser in *Globe and Mail Magazine* pp. 8-10, January 4, 1964.

"No End to Writing" - Editorial page, *Edmonton Journal,* April 7, 1964.

"Writing Essential" - Letter to editor of *Edmonton Journal* by Wilfred Watson, April 11, 1964.

"He Sees Paradise" - by Lee Belland, *Toronto Daily Star,* page 11, May 7, 1964.

May 11, 1964 - article in *Toronto Telegram.*

"Research Project with Awesome Implications" - Hugh Munro, *Globe & Mail,* May 9, 1964.

"Reverse Canadian" by Douglas Parker in *Parker's Bookshelf* Riverside California Press Enterprise, May 24, 1964.

Review of *Understanding Media* in *Sunday Herald Tribune,* Book Section, by Dwight Macdonald, June 7, 1964.

"Fame Can Frame You" in *Toronto Daily Star* (short article from Charlottetown) June 10, 1964.

"A Rich Sprawling Book" Review of *Understanding Media* by Arnold Rockman, *Toronto Daily Star,* June 13, 1964.

"Sights and Sounds" by Robert Russel, Review of *Understanding Media,* June 11, 1964. (no details)

"Keyhole TV" by Robert Davis - Letter to the Editor of *Toronto Daily Star,* June 13, 1964.

Review of *Gutenberg Galaxy* by Isabel McKenna in *The Bookshelf: Ottawa Public Library* - Sunday Radio Review CJET - CFRA - CFMO June 21, 1964.

"Today Our Brains are Outside our Skulls" by Arnold Rockman in Toronto Star, February 15, 1964.

"Born Under Telstar" - TIMES LITERARY SUPPLEMENT, Aug. 6, 1964, p. 693. Review of *Und. Media.*

"Out of the Tribe" by Ronald Hagler in BRITISH COL-UMBIA LIBRARY QUARTERLY, #28, July/Oct. 1964, p. 12.

Review of *Gutenberg Galaxy* in ANNALS OF THE AMERICAN ACADEMY OF POLITICAL AND SO-CIAL SCIENCE, #356 (Nov. 1964) p. 219. - by Pat Hazard.

"Reviews" by Dean Frye in RAMPARTS #3 (Oct. 1964) p. 63. Review of *Und. Media.*

"Big Dipper" by Rich. Hoggart in LISTENER, #72, Dec. 3, 1964, p. 895.

"The Cybernetic Caveman" by Deborah Holmes in NATION, #99, Oct. 5, 1964, p. 194. Review of *Und. Media.*

LAMP, 62 (Sept. 1964), page 16.

"Humpty-Dumpty in the Pushbutton Age" by Donald Mainwaring, in CHRISTIAN SCIENCE MONITOR (July 2, 1964), #7. Review of *Und. Media.*

"May 20 . . . McLuhan" - *KIRKUS* #32 (April 1, 1964) p. 394.

"McLuhan" by E.M. Oboler in LIBRARY JOURNAL #89 (June 1, 1964) 2359. Review of *Und. Media.*

"Change and the Invention of Printing" by James Reaney, *ETC* #21, December 1964, p. 495. Review of *Gut. Galaxy.*

"Electronic Man" by Christopher Ricks, NEW STATESMAN, #68 (Dec. 11, 1964) p. 925. Review of *Und. Media.*

"Mass Communications" by Campbell Sabiston in HUMANIST, #24, (Jan./Feb. 1964) p. 28. Review of *Gut. Galaxy.*

"Understanding Media" in VIRGINIA QUARTERLY REVIEW, #40 (Winter, 1964) p. 174. Rev. of *Und. Media.*

"Never Lose Your Cool" by Paul West, CANADIAN FORUM, #44 (Oct. 1964) p. 165. Review of *Und. Media.*

"Who is Marshall McLuhan?" in BRITISH COLUMBIA LIBRARY QUARTERLY, #28, (July-Oct. 1964) p. 3.

"A Structure of Insight" by Raymond Williams UNIVERSITY OF TORONTO QUARTERLY, #33 (Apr. 1964) p. 338. Rev. of *Gut. Galaxy.*

"Understanding Media: A McLuhan Sampler" in *Toronto Education Quarterly,* Vol. 111, #4, Summer, 1964, p. 17-21 (excerpts from *Understanding Media).*

"Rights for Translation into German of H.M. McLuhan's Gutenberg Galaxy sold to Walter-Verlag AG, Olten, Switzerland" in *Press* Notes, University of Toronto Press, Vol. VI, Nos. 6 and 7, June-July, 1964.

June 25, 1964 - article in *Toronto Telegram.*

June 30, 1964 - article in *Globe and Mail.*

July 3, 1964 - "Blowing Hot and Cold" - Review of *Understanding* Media, in *Time.*

Review of *Understanding Media* by Lister Sinclair, in *Globe and Mail,* July 11, 1964, page 13.

"McLuhan Explains the Media" by Dean Walker in *Executive Magazine* August, 1964, pp. 23-27.

Review of *Understanding Media* in *Times Literary Supplement,* August 6, 1964, page 693.

"How to Learn Economics in a Rowboat" by Ron Thompson, in *Toronto Star,* August 24, 1964, page 10.

"This is What They're Thinking" - by Tom Ford, in *Toronto Star* September 8, 1964, (Re Fredericton Conference)

"Dief in Beatle Wig? Yeah, Yeah, Yeah!" Special to the *Toronto Star* from Fredericton, September 10, 1964.

"Speaker Gives 200 Conservative Thinkers Something to Think About, But What?" - by Anthony Westell, *Toronto Globe and Mail,* September 10, 1964, page 1.

"Warns Bloody Revolt Could Kill French Canada Culture" by Tom Ford in *Toronto Star,* Sept. 10, 1964, p. 23.

Review of *Understanding Media* by James C. Nohrnberg (get details)

Review of *Understanding Media* by Chuck Bayley in *Vancouver Sun* September 4, 1964.

"Technology and Politics Aired" in *The Mail-Star* by Ken Kelly, September 10, 1964.

Review of *Gutenberg Galaxy* by Hugh D. Duncan in *Arts in Society* Vol. 3, #1, Sept. 17, 1964.

Review of *Understanding Media* by Ray Irwin in *Editor and Publisher* (850 Third Avenue, New York) Sept. 12, 1964.

Article re Fredericton Conference in *The Gazette* (Montreal) by Arthur Blakely, Sept. 10, 1964, pp. 1 and 7.

Article re Fredericton Conference in *Globe & Mail,* September 11, 1964.

Article on McLuhan in *Radio & TV Magazine,* by George Garlock September 8, 1964.

"The Medium Rules" article by Dennis Braithwaite in *Globe and Mail,* October 16, 1964.

Review of *Understanding Media* in *Commonweal Review* by C.J. Fox October 16, 1964.

"Understanding Marshall McLuhan" by Shelagh Lindsey in *British Columbia Library Quarterly,* Vol. 28, Nos. 1 and 2, Oct. 1964.

Article by Les Wedman in *Vancouver Sun,* November 3, 1964.

"The McLuhan Galaxy" by Russell Westkirk in *The Mike,* Vol. XVI, #10, November 20, 1964.

"Marshall McLuhan: Understanding Media" - in *Toronto Education Quarterly* Vol. 111, #4, Summer, 1964, pp. 17-21. (excerpts from the book)

"Misunderstanding Media" by Alan Thomas *The Telegram,* Aug. 22, 1964, p. 5.

"In Sight" by Dean Walker - "McLuhan Stalks the Sensory Pathways" in *Marketing Magazine,* January 1, 1965.

Review of *Understanding Media* by Harold Rosenberg in *The New Yorker* February 27, 1965.

"Video: The World Becomes a Village" by R.J. Childerhouse in *The Toronto Telegram,* March 1, 1965.

"McLuhan Lecture" by Daniel John Zimmerman in *The Spectrum,* Buffalo March 6, 1965. (re Prof. McLuhan's lecture at Univ. of New York at Buffalo on March 5th).

"The High Priest of Pop Culture" by Alexander Ross in *Macleans Magazine,* July 3, 1965, pp. 13 and 42-43.

"A Lost Cause" by Larry Elliott in the *Edmonton Journal* - TV Views Column, April, 1965.

Review of *Understanding Media* by Dubarry Campo, in *Toronto Telegram* May 22, 1965, p. 43 and 44.

"Lunching at Off-Broadway in North Beach with McLuhan, Tom Wolfe, Adman, Howard Gossage and Dr. Gerald Feigen" by Herb Caen in *San Francisco Chronicle,* Aug. 12, 1965.

A Review of *Understanding Media* by Kenneth Winetrout - "McLuhan: Gutenberg Mortician and Electronic Prophet" in *The Torch,* Vol. 111, Spring Issue, 1965, American International College, Springfield, Mass. - pp. 29-30.

"Philosophy in a Pop Key" by Harold Rosenberg, *The New Yorker,* Feb. 27, 1965, pp. 192-135.

"The High Priest of Pop Culture" by Alexander Ross, *McLean's Magazine,* July 7, 1965, pp. 13, 42-43.

"Marshall McLuhan: Canada's Intellectual Comet" - Richard Schickel *Harper's* - Nov. 1965, pp. 183-184.

"Burroughs" by Michael Smith - *Nation* #200 (Jan. 11, 1965), p. 21.

"Advertising: A Different Look at Creativity" - *New York Times* September 8, 1965.

"The McLuhan Galaxy" by Jerome B. Agel in *Books,* New York, Vol. 2, #8 pp. 1-3 - September, 1965 (598 Madison Avenue).

"Marshall McLuhan, Prophet and Analyst of the Age of Instant Knowledge: Easing the Technological Burden of Western man" article in *Canada Month* by John Kettle - pp. 10-12, October, 1965.

Review of *Understanding Media* by Tony Hodgkinson in *Bostonia* Magazine (University of Boston - we have no copy).

"The New Life Out There" article by Tom Wolfe, in *New York Herald* magazine, Sunday, November 21, 1965.

November, 1965 - article in *Harper's* magazine - we do not have copy.

"Did You Know?" by Roy Shields in *Toronto Daily Star,* November 23, 1965.

"La Comete Intellectuelle Du Canada" article by Naim Kattan in *Le Devoir,* Montreal, November 27, 1965.

Review of *Gutenberg Galaxy* and *Understanding Media* appeared in *Critique,* Paris, France - articles done by Paul Riesman, Dec. 1965.

"He Says Politicians Should Copy the Beatles" - Peter C. Newman *Toronto Daily Star,* page 7, December 1965.

1965-1966 - *Main Currents In Modern Thought* (Julius Stulman, Publisher) - Review of *Gutenberg Galaxy,* Volume 22, pages 52-58.

Review of *Understanding Media* by Sam. Becker in QUARTERLY JOURNAL OF SPEECH, #51 (Feb. 1965, p. 86.

"Paradise Regained or McLuhancy" by Jack Behar and Lieberman in TEACHER'S COLLEGE RECORD, #64 (April 1965) p. 645.

"The Medium is the Message" by Ken Boulding in CANADIAN JOURNAL OF ECONOMICS AND POLITICAL SCIENCE, #31 (May 1965) p. 268. Review of *Gut. Galaxy.*

"The Cool Rev." by Neil Compton in COMMENTARY, #39 (Jan. 1965), pp. 79-81. Review of *Und. Media.*

"LSD: The Contact High" by Howard Junker in NATION, #201 (July 5, 1965) p. 25.

Review of *Understanding Media* by Richard Kostelanetz in COMMONWEAL #83, December 3, 1965, p. 286.

"For High School Classrooms" by Homer Marshfield, in SPIRIT, #32 (Nov. 1965) p. 129, Rev. of *Voices of Literature.*

"Advertisers Shy from Culture Tag" - an interview by James Peters, Assistant Registrar at Ryerson appeared in *Canadian Broadcaster,* Volume 24, #10 - Radio Station CJRT-FM Broadcast facility of Ryerson Polytechnical Institute. - May 27, 1966.

"The Talk of the Town" column of *The New Yorker* - May 25, 1966 item: "The McLuhan Metaphor" p. 43 and 44.

"Any Number Can Play" by David Cort, Book Review Section *New York Times,* May 1, 1966.

"Hello Electric Age" by Eliot Fremont-Smith in "Books of the Times" *New York Times* May 11, 1966 (re Y.M.H.A. appearance on May 7, 1966).

"Advertisers Shy from Culture Tag" by Frank Kelley in *Canadian Broadcaster,* May 27, 1966 (Volume 24, #10).

"Spectre of Obsolescence" by Clarence Peterson - Review of *Understanding Media* in Chicago Tribune, May 29, 1966, p. 9.

"The Child of the Future: How He Might Learn" in *Film News* by editor, Rohama Lee (re film Sept. 19, 1965 produced by Ted Conant for the National Film Board of Canada) April, 1966.

B.B.C. News Headlines in *The Listener,* Vol. LXXXV, #1939, London, England - "We and Us" p. 748 re B.B.C. Third Program. May 26, 1966.

"Electric Assault" by Paul Ferris in *The Observer,* London, England, May 29, 1966.

Article by Ruth Cohen in *Canadian University magazine,* Vol. 1, #2, pp. 33-34 and 46 - May/June issue, 1966.

"The Doubtful Necessity of Understanding McLuhan" by Ross Wetzsteon in *The Village Voice* (Greenwich Village paper) May 12, 1966.

"Understanding McLuhan" by Howard Gossage in *Madison Avenue* (Advertising magazine, monthly, 575 Madison Avenue, New York) June, 1966 - pp. 28-29, 52-43 and 62.

"The McLuhan Effect" by Robert L. Shayon in *Saturday Review* (TV & Radio section) June 4, 1966.

"The Brave New World of Marshall McLuhan in *Glamour Magazine,* pp. 100 and 133-135, July 1966.

"If You Ask Me" by Earl Lifshey in *Home Furnishings Daily,* Chicago (re National Housewares Manufacturing Association design awards talk on July 11, 1966) July 18, 1966.

An article on Prof. McLuhan by Mark L. Krupnick in *The Church* (17 Dunster St., Cambridge, Mass.) February 1966, pp. 10 and 11.

Article by Mr. Pollock in *Newsweek* Magazine, Feb. 25, 1966, pp. 56-57.

Long article about Prof. McLuhan (with pictures) in *Life* magazine February 28, 1966, pp. 91-99.

"Is Technology Taking Over" in *Fortune* Magazine, February 1966, p. 112.

*New York Times Magazine* - article about the "Joan Baez school for non-violent resisters in California . . . discuss their reading: Gandhi, Thoreau, McLuhan," etc. (1st week of March).

Article by McKenzie Porter in *Toronto Daily Star*, Feb. 18, 1966, p. 12.

"Students Read Lewis Carroll - McLuhan stages a 'colossal Happening' to teach poetry" - (re taping-Elwy Yost CBC) appeared in *Toronto Daily Star, March 7, 1966*.

Taped interview by Bob Davis in *Varsity News* (U of T) March issue, 1966.

"Marshall McLuhan — the man who infuriates the critics" by Thos. P. McDonnell in *U.S. Catholic Magazine* - pp. 27-32 - March, 1966. (221 W. Madison Avenue, Chicago, Illinois).

"TV Turns Westerners Into Orientals" says author - *Washington Post* April 4, 1966.

"TV Seen Making Bit Changes in Culture" by Lawrence Laurent in *Los Angeles Times,* April 4, 1966.

"Understanding McLuhan" by Howard Gossage - *Ramparts* Magazine, April, 1966.

"Goodbye to Gutenberg" Special science report in *Newsweek,* Jan. 24, 1966, page 85.

"Harold Adams Innis and Marshall McLuhan" - a paper read by James W. Carey at Association for Education in Journalism Convention in Iowa City, Aug. 28-Sept. 3, 1966.

"I Met the Oracle of the Electronic Age" by Paul Grescoe, *Toronto Telegram,* July 23, 1966.

"TV Turns Westerners Into Orientals, Author Says" - *Washington Post,* April 4, 1966, A-10.

"Magazines: a Private War" by Robert Fulford, in *Toronto Star* p. 31, March 3, 1966.

"A Hard Look at Canada's Cultural Hero" by Benjamin DeMott in *Esquire Magazine,* July, 1966.

"Pop People Take Over" by Robert Fulford, in *Toronto Daily Star* July 22, 1966. (Mr. Fulford argues that DeMott is attacking McLuhan's attitudes rather than his ideas.)

"The World and Marshall McLuhan" by Eric Mottram in *Journal of Canadian Studies* - Volume 1, #2, pp. 37-54, August, 1966 (Trent University, Peterborough).

"Utopianism, Alienation and Marshall McLuhan" by David Sheps in *Canadian Dimensions Magazine* (P.O. Box 1413, Winnipeg, Man.) Volume 3, #6, pp. 23-26, Sept./Oct. 1966.

"Understanding McLuhan? It's Worth a Try" by Rolf Pedersen in *Brandon Sun,* Manitoba, Oct. 15, 1966.

"McLuhanism: Is the Medium Getting the Message?" by Frank Tyler Television Magazine (1735 DeSales St. N.W. Washington D.C.) Volume XXIII, #12, pp. 35-37 and 66-69, December 1966.

"Marshall McLuhan Wins Schweitzer Award - $100,000" in *Toronto* Star, December 30, 1966.

Small paper "From the Editorial Desk" - article: "Understanding McLuhan: The Extensions of Innis" by Edgar A. Grunwald (formerly managing editor of *Business Week)* sponsored by Union Carbide Corp., December, 1966.

Review of Gutenberg Galaxy in *Main Currents in Modern Thought* Vo. 22, 1965-66, pp. 52-58. (December, 1966).

"Folklore of Electrical Man: Marshall McLuhan" by Raymond Waddington in *New Mexico Quarterly* - Fall issue, 1966, p. 241-257.

"Understanding McLuhan" by Edward Wakin, in *Sign* Magazine, January, 1967 - pp. 28-32.

Panel Discussion on Marshall McLuhan: General Semanticists View his Ideas on Culture, Education, Media - On panel: Raymond Arlo, Ronald Gross, Harry Maynard, Charles Weingartner, Oct. 19, 1966 in Carnegie Endowment Bldg. 345 East 56th St., New York City.

"Understanding McLuhan" by Hugh Kenner in *National Review,* Nov. 29, 1966, pp. 1224-1225.

"McLuhanism Reconsidered" by Eric Barnouw in *Saturday Review*, July 23, 1966, pp. 19-21.

"Oracle of the Electric Age" by Jane Howard in *Life*, Feb. 28, 1966, pp. 91-99.

"Is Technology Taking Over?" by Chas. E. Silberman, *Fortune*, Feb. 1966, pp. 112-115, and 212-222.

McLuhanism: Is the Medium Getting the Message?" by Ralph Tyler, Television, Dec. 1966, pp. 35-37 and 66-69.

"Link-Beaming: Overcoming Social Lags in Teaching Transitional Disciplines by the Projection of Expansible Programs" by Dr. Henry G. Burger, Anthropologist (Dept. Sociology, Univ. Mo. Kansas City, Mo. 64110) in *International Journal of Educational Science, Vol. 2*, pp. 201-208 (Pergamon Press Limited, 1966, Great Britain).

Article by McKenzie Porter in *Toronto Daily Star*, Feb. 18, 1966, p. 12.

"Students Read Carroll - McLuhan Stages 'A Colossal Happening'" *Toronto Daily Star*, March 7, 1966, p. 17.

"Creativity and Commitment" by Ed Albee in SATURDAY REVIEW, #49, June 4, 1966, p. 26.

"Medium as Message" by Kenneth Burke in LANGUAGE AS SYMBOLIC ACTION, 1966, p. 410.

"Howdy, Neighbor" by James Burnham in NATIONAL REVIEW, #18, (Oct. 4, 1966, p. 976.

"Why a Newspaper in an Electronic Era" by Otis Chandler, in NIEMAN REPORTS #20, (Dec. 1966), p. 8-9.

Article by Ruth Cohen in CANADIAN UNIVERSITY MAGAZINE, 1 No. 2, (May/June 1966) pp. 33-34.

"Marshall McLuhan and the Ad Man" by Bernard Davies, in AD WEEKLY (Dec. 30, 1966).

"The Message of Marshall McLuhan" by Barry Day in *Advertising Quarterly*, No. 8 (Summer, 1966).

"King of Popthink" by Benjamin DeMott in *Esquire* (Aug. 1966) p. 71.

"Marshall McLuhan: Double Agent" by G.P. Elliott, in *Public Interest* No. 4 (Summer, 1966) p. 116.

"Prophet of What?" by Robert Fulford, in *The Observer* (United Church), Nov. 15, 1966, page 15.

"Book Review: Understanding Media" by Anthony W. Hodgkinson *Boston University School of Public Communication Alumni News*, 1, No. 15, (Feb. 28, 1966) p. 4.

"An Architecture for the Electronic Age" by John M. Johanson in *American Scholar*, 35 (Spring, 1966), p. 461.

"Advertisers Shy from Cultural Tag" by Frank Kelley, *Canadian Broadcaster*, 24, No. 10 (May 27, 1966) p. 9.

"The Cool Totalitarian" by Chris Koch, in *Ramparts*, 5 (Oct. 1966), p. 55. Review of *Understanding Media*.

"McLuhan: A Hot Apostle in a Cool Culture" by Richard Kostelanetz in *Twentieth Century Magazine*, 175 (Autumn 1966), p. 38.

"Books in Review" by T.S. May in *Journal of Broadcasting*, X, Spring, 1966, p. 183. Review of *Gutenberg Galaxy* and *Understanding Media*.

"McLuhan Malady" in *Printer's Ink*, 292 (December 9, 1966), p. 68.

"Questions and Answers with McLuhan" in *Take One* magazine, Nos. 1 and 2 (Nov., Dec., 1966).

"The Changing Role of Man" by Wesley Meirhenry, in *Educational Screen and Audiovisual Guide* (March, 1966), p. 27.

"What Nature Abhors" - The Nation-Editorial Staff, in *Nation*, 203 (December, 1966) p. 596.

"The Electronic Prophet" by Kathleen Nott, in *The Observer* (London) August 7, 1966.

"Our Times" - *Saturday Review,* 49 (December 17, 1966), p. 37.

"Medium is the Message" by Harley Parker in *Educational Screen and Audiovisual Guide,* March, 1966, p. 26. Review of *Understanding Media.*

"People" - *Time,* 87 (June 24, 1966), p. 48.

"People" - *Time,* 87 (Dec. 2, 1966), p. 46.

*Books Today,* by C. Peterson, (December, 1966), p. 35.

"People Are Talking About . . ." - *Vogue,* 148 (July, 1966), p. 60.

"McLuhan Is the Message" by Chas. K. Raymond, in *Journal of Advertising Research,* 6 (June, 1966), p. 68.

"The Summa Popologica of Marshall McLuhan" by Theodore Rozak in *New Politics,* 5 (Fall, 1966), p. 22.

"This Time of Year" by Rollene W. Saal, in *Saturday Review,* 49 (Nov. 26, 1966), p. 40.

"Old Wine in New Bottles" by Tony Schwartz, in *Popular Photography,* 69 (Nov. 1966), p. 50.

"The McLuhan Effect" by Robt. L. Shayon, in *Saturday Review,* 49, (June 4, 1966), p. 54.

**1966 -
1967**

"Artist and/in the Electronic Environment" by Dido Smith, in *Craft Horizon* 26 (Nov. - Dec. 1966), p. 42.

"McLuhanism" by Moira Walsh, in *America,* 114 (May 28, 1966), p. 784.

"What Nature Abhors" in *Nation* (Dec. 5, 1966), p. 596.

Review of film *The Child of the Future: How He Might Learn* by Stephanie Simon in *Film News magazine* (film produced by N.F.B. of Canada, 1966).

"Unhappy Media" by Ken Allsop in *Punch* 253 (Oct. 4, 1967), p. 520. Review of *Understanding Media, The Medium is the Massage, Mechanical Bride* and *Gutenberg Galaxy.*

"McLuhan" by Alvin Balk in *Saturday Review*, 50 (March 11, 1967), p. 137.

"Architecture in the Electronic Age by Jonathan Barnett - *Architectural Record*, 141 (March, 1967), p. 151.

*Books Today* - L. Bridges (IV - May 28, 1967), p. 14.

"Child's Guide to McLology" by Alan Brien in *New Statesman*, 73 (Feb. 10, 1967), p. 187.

"The Modicum is the Message" by Anthony Burgess in *Spectator*, 219 (Oct. 13, 1967), p. 427.

"Flowering Paradox: McLuhan Newark" by Alan D. Coleman in *Village Voice* (Sept. 28, 1967), p. 23-24.

"Sex and the Western World: McLuhan's Misunderstanding" by James L. Collier in *Village Voice* (Sept. 7, 1967), page 3.

"A Pot of Message" by Neil Compton, in *Nation*, 204 (May 15, 1967), p. 63. Review of *The Medium is the Massage*.

"McLuhanite Christianity at Expo 67" by Harvey Cox in *Commonweal* 86 (May 26, 1967), p. 277.

"Clue to McLuhan" by Barry Day, in *Ad Weekly*, (Sept. 29, 1967).

"McLuhan" by H.W. Dillon in *Library Journal*, 98 (June 1, 1967) 2172. Review of *Medium is the Massage*.

"Understanding McLuhan" by John Duncan in *Listener*, 78 (Oct. 19, 1967), p. 493.

"About Marshall McLuhan: Who Said TV Had to Make Sense" by Stanley Frank in *TV Guide* (May 13, 1967), pp. 8-11.

"With all the Stops Out" by Michael Frayn in *The Observer* (London) June 11, 1967.

"Thoughts of Chairman McLuhan" by Philip French in *London Financial Times*, Oct. 5, 1967.

Article about Prof. McLuhan by Richard Kostelanetz in *Commonweal* Magazine, January 20, 1967.

"Understanding McLuhan (in part)" by Richard Kostelanetz in *New York Times,* Section 6, pp. 18-19 and 37-50, January 29, 1967.

"Understanding Canada and other Sundry Matters: Marshall McLuhan" *Madamoiselle Magazine* (Mary Winocour, Feature Editor, 420 Lexington Avenue, N.Y. 10017) pp. 114-115 and 126-130. January, 1967.

"A Cool Look at What Marshall McLuhan's Getting At" by Robert Fulford, in *Toronto Daily Star,* January 21, 1967, pp. 23-25.

"Marshall McLuhan - Media Mastermind" in 'On the Scene' section *Playboy* magazine, p. 142, February, 1967.

"Canadians are unaware of most everything" by John LeBlanc, *St. Catharines Standard,* p. 30, Jan. 18, 1967.

"Cover Story - Home Entertainment" pp. 30-32 and 37-39, *Forbes* magazine, March 15, 1967. (magazine cover drawing by Rube Goldberg).

"The Message of Marshall McLuhan" in Newsweek (with cover photo), March 6, 1967 - pp. 53-57.

"A Schoolman's Guide to Marshall McLuhan" by John M. Culkin, S.J. in *Saturday Review* - p. 51, March 18, 1967. (cover photo by Karsh).

"Get the Message?" review of *The Medium is the Massage* - by Marvin Kitman in *The New York Times Book Review* - p. 6 and 7, March 26, 1967.

"McLuhan Makes his Point with Brilliant TV Style" article by Louise Sweeney in *The Christian Science Monitor,* p. 4, Mar. 20, 1967.

"Alone in the Global Village" - Ralph Hancox, editor *The Peterborough Examiner,* p. 4, March 22, 1967.

March, 1967 - *Kenyon Review* article (do not have copy)

Spring 1967 - *Antioch Review* (do not have copy).

"Marshall McLuhan: Communications Explorer" in *America* Magazine article by Neil P. Hurley (America Press Inc., 106 W. 56th St., New York N.Y. 10019) pp. 241-243.

"McLuhan's Views Reshape Museum" by John M. Lee in Globe & Mail, February 23, 1967.

February, 1967 - article in *Saturday Night* - (do not have copy).

"Something of Marshall McLuhan" by Jonathan Fox appeared in *Comment* (New Zealand periodical - do not have copy).

"McLuhan and Parish Pastors by William C. Henzlik, in *Christian* Advocate, Vol. XI, #9, published by The Methodist Publishing House, 201-8th Avenue S., Nashville, Tenn. 37203. p. 7-9, May, 1967.

"Back Talk" by Edwin G. Schwenn, editor *The American Press,* May 1967, Vol. 85, #7, p. 58 (1215 Wilmette Avenue, Wilmette, Illinois 60091).

"Exploring with McLuhan" by John M. Culkin, S.J. in *College and University Journal,* Spring, 1967, Vol. 6, #2, p. 8-9.

"Communication Expert Scorns Electronic Media" by John R. Sullivan, in *The Catholic News* (N.Y. newspaper) on page 9, June 1, 1967.

"McLuhan is the Massage" in *The Alumni Journal,* University of Manitoba, Vol. 27, #3, Spring issue, 1967, pp. 21-22.

Biography of Marshall McLuhan appeared in *Current Biography* (The H.W. Wilson Company, N.Y.) Vol. 28, #6, June, 1967, pp. 20-22.

"3,000 See SFU Tune-in, Turn-on" - article in *The Vancouver Sun* May 23, 1967, p. 14. (re convocation ceremonies at Simon Fraser University where Prof. McLuhan was guest speaker and received an honorary doctrate).

"Sex and the Western World: McLuhan's Misunderstanding" by James L. Collier in *Village Voice* (Sept. 7, 1967), page 3.

"Personality of the Year" in *Collier's 1967 Year Book* covering the year 1966 - Corwell Collier and Macmillan Inc. 1967, p. 399.

"McLuhanism in a Nutshell - The Dangers of a Theory" in *The Gazette* (Montreal) article by Louis Dudek - April 8, 1967, p. 28.

"The Gutenberg Hang-up or Linear Heads Among the Squares or Rummaging Around the McLoony Bin" - in *The Washington* magazine, Vol. 2, #10, July, 1967 - article by Tom Donnelly pp. 36-50. (1218 Connecticut Avenue, Washington, D.C. 20036).

"Le Prophete De L'Information - Science & Vie" - Daniel Garric, in *Arsene Okun,* Vol. 67, #599, Aug. 1967, pp. 24-29.

September, 1967 - *Antioch Review* article (do not have copy)

"Council Awards Distinguished Canadians" article re Molson award in Vancouver, *Toronto Star,* Oct. 16, 1967.

Cartoon in *Look* magazine - Two natives - one says: "And then when I finally *did* talk my tribe into learning to read, they read Marshall McLuhan!"

"Harold Adams Innis and Marshall McLuhan" by James W. Carey - *Antioch Review,* Fall, 1967.

"Like Yoga, Not Like the Movies" - *Forbes Magazine,* 99 (Mar. 15, 1967), p. 40.

"Medium is the Message from McLuhan" - *Catholic World Herald Citizen* (Feb. 18, 1967), p. 19.

"McLuhan Montage" - *Library Journal* 92 (April 15, 1967), p. 1701.

"McLuhan the Medium" by Kenneth Melvin, *Phi Delta Kappan,* 58 (June 1967), p. 488.

"The LSS Syndrome, Principles and Heresies" by Frank Meyer - *National Review,* XIX (Mar. 21, 1967), p. 301.

"The Medium is the Medium: Principles and Heresies" by Frany Meyer - *National Review* XIX (April 18, 1967), p. 119.

"The Medium is McLuhan" by Malcolm Muggeridge in *New Statesman* 74 (Sept. 1, 1967), p. 253.

"Review of *The Medium is the Massage*" by Malcolm Muggeridge - *Esquire,* 68 (Aug. 1967), p. 14.

"Into McLuhan's Maelstrom" by Tom Nairn in *New Statesman,* 74, (Sept. 22, 1967), p. 362. Review of *Mechanical Bride, Und. Media, Gutenberg Galaxy* and *Medium is the Massage.*

"What Is McLuhan Saying - Is the Medium Really the Message?" by Fred Pearson in *Eternity Magazine,* 18 (Oct. 1967), p. 20.

"The Channel and the Signs" by Octavio Pag in his *Alternating Current.* 1967.

"The 'Quality' Books" by Clarence Peterson - *Book World,* 1 (Oct. 8, 1967), p. 17.

"Programming Getting the Message" - *Time* (Oct. 13, 1967), p. 47.

"McLuhan's Tom-Tom" by Raymond Rosenthal in *New Leader,* 50 (May 8, 1967), p. 22. Review of *Medium is the Massage.*

"Not-So-Cool McLuhan" by Robt. Shayon in *Saturday Review,* 50 (Apr. 15, 1967), p. 46.

"Speaking of Holiday, The Importance of Being Different" - *Holiday* 42 (Oct. 1967), p. 37.

"The Future For" by Chas. A. Sprague in *Nieman Report,* 21 (Sept. 1967), pp. 9-12.

"On Reading Marshall McLuhan" by Geo. Steiner in his *Language and Silence,* 1967.

"The Medium" by J. Thompson, - *Spectator,* 219 (Sept. 8, 1967), p. 270.

"The Ultimate Non-Book" - *Time,* 88 (Mar. 3, 1967, p. 102. Review of *Medium is the Massage.*

"Protestant Man on the Brink of Extinction" by Robt. Fulford in *United Church Herald* (Jan. 1967), p. 9.

"Graphics Convey Message in *Medium is the Massage*" - *Publisher's Weekly,* 191 (April 3, 1967) p. 62. Review of *Medium is the Massage.*

*Manchester Guardian* - article by Martin Green, #97 (Oct. 5, 1967), p. 10.

"Is McLuhan A Medium?" by Martin Green in *Commonweal,* 84 (June 23, 1967), p. 395.

"Media Man's Mascot" by Martin Green, in *Guardian* (Sept. 28, 1967).

"Breaking Bread With the Wizard of Oz" by Richard Goldstein, in *Village Voice* (June 1, 1967), pp. 12-13.

"A Cool View of McLuhan" by Hamar-Brown - in *Advertising Quarterly,* No. 12 (Summer, 1967).

"Marshall McLuhan" by Alfred Heintz in *The Australian* (Melbourne) Oct. 14, 1967.

"Last Words" by Christopher Hollis, in *Spectation* 219 (Oct. 13, 1967), p. 419.

"The Tree Universities" by Ralph Keyes, in *Nation,* 205 (Oct. 2, 1967), p. 294.

"The Message is McLuhan" by Rudolph Klein in *Observer* (United Church) (Oct. 1, 1967), p. 9.

"Marshalling McLuhanism" by Arthur Knight in *Saturday Review,* 50 (Aug. 12, 1967), p. 42.

"The Hidden Dimension" by Richard Kostelanetz - *Twentieth Century Magazine,* 174, No. 1035 (1967/8), p. 48.

"McLuhan's Own Trot" by Richard Kostelanetz in *Reporter*, 34 (April 20, 1967), p. 52. Review of *The Medium is the Massage*.

"If You Don't Mind My Saying So . . ." by Joseph W. Krutch in *American Scholar*, 36 (Autumn 1967), p. 532.

"Book of the Month" by Daniel J. Leary in *Catholic World*, 205 (June 1967), p. 177. Review of *Medium is the Massage*.

"Voices of Convergence: Teilhard, McLuhan, and Brown" by Daniel J. Leary, in *Catholic World* 204 (Jan. 1967), p. 206.

"Media: Linear, Electric, and Square" by Robt. Lekachman, in *Harpers*, 234 (June 1967), p. 103. Review of *Medium is the Massage*.

"McLuhan: The Abominable Snowman" - by David Myers, *Chicago Tribune* Book World, Oct. 29, 1967, p. 25.

"Are Marshall McLuhan's Statements Logical or Clear, or Factual, or Consistent, or Correct" by Robt. Fulford, *Chicago Tribune Magazine* June 11, 1967, p. 48.

"New Sage Rather Boxed Up" by Chas. Curran, *London Sunday Telegram*, Oct. 1, 1967.

"An Electronic Gadfly's Communications Ideas" by Robt. Kirsh, *Los Angeles Times Calender* (March 12, 1967), p. 30.

"Why Marshall McLuhan Matters to You" by Thomas Ralph, *Toronto Daily Star* (January 21, 1967), page 25.

"McLuhanism" by Christopher Ricks, in LISTENER, #78 (Sept. 1967) p. 386. Review of *The Medium is the Massage*.

1967-
1968    "McLuhan: A Pretentious Pastische" by Thos. Lask, *New York Times*, Sept. 10, 1967, p. 30D

"Book of the Month: The Medium is the Massage" by Daniel J. Leary *Catholic World*, June 1967, pp. 177-178.

"McLuhan Montage" - *Library Journal,* April 15, 1967, pp. 1701-1703.

"The Medium is the Medium: Principles and Heresies" by Frank S. Meyer *National Review,* April 18, 1967, p. 419.

"McLuhan: The Abominable Snowman" by David Myers, *Chicago Tribune Book World,* Oct. 29, 1967, p. 25.

"Programming: Getting the Message" - *Time,* Oct. 13, 1967, p. 47.

"The Plugged-in Generation" Arthur Schlesinger, Jr. *World Journal Tribune Book Week,* March 19, 1967, pp. 1-2.

"The McLuhan Myth" by Chas. Steinberg, *Television Quarterly,* VI, #3, 1967, p. 7-15.

"McLuhanism: Understanding Marshall's Media" by Christopher Sterling (Unpublished paper, Dept. of Speech, Univ. of Wisconsin, 1967) (Mimeographed).

"The Last (The Very Last" Word on Marshall McLuhan" by Ralph Thomas in *Chicago Tribune Sunday Magazine,* June 11, 1967, pp. 28-29, 43-46.

"Understanding Marshall McLuhan or Will TV Put a Zombie in Your Future" *Senior Scholastic,* XC, No. 12, 1967, p. 13-16.

"An All-at-Onceness Teach-in: McLuhan Hot and Cool" by Dudley Young *New York Times Book Review,* Nov. 19, 1967, p. 4.

"McLuhan: The Myth of the Powerhouse" by John Quirk in *The Activist* Activist Pub. Co. Ltd., Oberlin, Ohio. pp. 7-8, 36-40.

"The Message of Marshall McLuhan" Special report by *Newsweek* March 6, 1967, pp. 53-57. Cover photo of McLuhan, and pic. of family.

chapter in book

"Marshall McLuhan: High Priest of the Electronic Village" - chapter in *Master Minds* by Richard Kostelanetz published by The MacMillan Company, Toronto, 1967 -

"Marshall McLuhan" - by Richard Kostelanetz in *Commonweal*, January 20, 1967, pp. 420 to 426.

"A Guide to McLuhan" by John Culkin, Nov.-Dec. issue of *Religious Education*, The Religious Education Association, New York City, 1968.

Review of *The Mechanical Bride, The Gutenberg Galaxy* and *Understanding Media* by Malcolm Griffith and Earl Seidman, Univ. of Washington appeared in *College Composition and Communication*, Feb. 1968. (no details) (draft in file).

"Metaphysician of Media" by C. Kenneth Johnstone in *Edge 6*, Spring, 1967 published by the Univ. of Edmonton, Alta. pp. 120-4.

"Marshall McLuhan" by Harry J. Boyle in *Telegram Weekend Magazine* Vol. 17, #11, March 18, 1967, pp. 2-9. (picture of McLuhan and Harley Parker on front cover).

"A Catholic Galaxy in 'Orange' Toronto" by Allen Spraggett, *Star,* Jan. 7, 1967 (p. 61).

"How to keep up? Just stay ahead" by Kildare Dobbs in *Toronto Star* Sept. 17, 1968, p. 26.

*McLuhan Hot and Cool* edited by Gerald E. Stearn, New York: Dial Press, 1967.

"Marshall McLuhan and the Technological Embrace" *The New Yorker* April 15, 1967, pp. 135-138, written by Michael Arlen.

"Architecture in the Electronic Age" by Jonathan Barnett, in Architectural Record, March, 1967, pp. 151-152.

"Harold Adams Innis and Marshall McLuhan, by James W. Carey, *Antioch Review*, XXVII, #1 (1967) p. 5-39.

"A Schoolman's Guide to Marshall McLuhan" by John Culkin, S.J. in *Saturday Review*, March 8, 1967, pp. 51-53, 70-72. Cover photo of McLuhan.

"The Message of Marshall McLuhan" by Edwin DeMott, in *Newsweek,* March 6, 1967, pp. 53-57.

"Are Marshall McLuhan's Statements Logical, or Clear, or Factual, or Consistent, or Correct" by Robert Fulford in *Chicago Tribune Sunday Magazine,* June 11, 1967, pp. 48-51.

"Who's Afraid of Marshall McLuhan" by Pete Hamil, in *Cosmopolitan,* Dec. 1967, pp. 82-85 and 149.

"Unravelling McLuhan" by Anthony Hodgkinson, in *Screen Education* 37, London: Society for Education in Film and Television, 1967.

"Marshall McLuhan: Communications Explorer" by Neil Hurley *America,* Feb. 18, 1967, pp. 241-243.

"Understanding McLuhan (In Part)" by Richard Kostelanetz, *New York Times Magazine,* Jan. 29, 1967, pp. 18-19, 37, 40, 42, 44, 47.

ook   *Sense and Nonsense of McLuhan* by Sidney Finkelstein, International, N.Y. 1968.

"Unhappy Medium" - *Economist,* 224 (Sept. 30, 1967), p. 1201. Review of *Und. Media, Mech. Bride, Gut. Galaxy, Medium is the Massage.*

"Misunderstanding Media: Obscurity As Authority" by Geoffrey Wagner, - *Kenyon Review,* 29 (Mar. 1967), p. 246.

"McLuhan Explains the Media" by Dean Walker, *Executive* (Toronto) August, 1964.

"I Read You Loud and Clear" by Lewis L. Wilkins - *Student World,* 60 (Third Quarter, 1967), p. 278.

"The Medium is the Message" by Duane D. Angel - *Quarterly Journal of Speech,* 54 (April, 1968), p. 194. Review of *Medium is the Massage.*

"McLuhan's Finnegans Wake" by Jack Behar - *Denver Quarterly,* 111 (Spring 1968), pp. 5-27.

"Levres En Francais" by Jean Benefant - *University of Toronto Quarterly,* 38 (July 1968), p. 489.

"The Death of Sequence: A Partial Defense of McLuhan" by Jerry Bowles - Cimaron Review, 1 (March, 1968), pp. 55-57.

"Reading, Writing, and McLuhan" by David Bronson - *English Journal* 52 (Nov. 1968), p. 1151.

"The Politics of the Electronic Revolution: Further Notes on Marshall McLuhan" by James Carey - Paper presented to the A.E.J. Convention, Lawrence, Kansas, 1968.

"McLuhan" by M.B. Cassata - *Library Journal* 93 (Nov. 1, 1968), 4126. Review of *War and Peace in the Global Village*.

"McLuhan" by G.A. Cevasco - *Library Journal* 93 (Nov. 1, 1968), 4130. Review of *Through the Vanishing Point*.

"The Paradox of Marshall McLuhan" by Neil Compton - *New American Review* No. 2, (Jan. 1968), p. 77.

"Marshall McLuhan's Theory of Sensory Form" by W. Comstock *Soundings,* 51 (Summer, 1968), p. 166.

"Marshall McLuhan, A Massager With a Message" by Porter Crow, *Journal of Thought,* 3 (Nov. 1968), p. 298.

"The Lonely Frontier of Reason" by Michael Crozier, - *Nation,* 204 (May 27, 1968), p. 690.

"Too Hot Not To Cool Down" by Barry Day - *Sight and Sound,* 37 (Spring, 1968), p. 28.

**1968** "Wenn der Botschafter zur Botschaft wird" by Von Georg Ramseger in *Handelsblatt,* February 1, 1968, Germany (newspaper).

Book *The McLuhan Explosion* - Harry H. Crosby and George R. Bond, American Book Company, 1968, New York.

"Marshall McLuhan and Italic Handwriting" by Lloyd Reynolds in *The Journal of the Society for Italic Handwriting* 56 (Fall, 1968), pp. 12-18.

"Marshalling the Clues" - A paper presented to the British Society of Aesthetics, Royal College of Art, Kensington Gore, London SW 7, England, on January 1, 1968. (24 pages). Prepared and read by Prof. C.H. Cornford.

*McLuhan: Pro and Con* (essays) - Funk, 1968.

Summer, 1968 - *Partisan Review* (do not have copy)

"McLuhan Sees Schools in Flames" - *Tornoto Star CP* (comments of Prof. McLuhan at gatheeeering after he gave a speech at the Inn-on-the Park on May 29, 1968 appeared in *Star* on May 30, 1968).

"PM Like Indian Mask - Stanfield a 'Trader'" - Glen Allen article re "Great Debate" program quotes McLuhan in *Toronto Star,* June 11, 1968, pp. 1 and 4.

"Great Debate: First came the egg, then came the omlet" by Roy Shields in *Tornoto Star,* Tues. June 11, p. 24 (re Great Debate analysis).

"Marshall McLuhan estuda um vilarejo chamado Mundo" - full page article on HMM appeared in *Diario de Pernambuco - Domingo* by Teresa Lucia Halliday (p. 13) January 14, 1968. (Her address: Rua Henrique Dias, 81 - Bon Vista, Recife, Pe. Brasil).

Sept. 8, 1968 - *New York Times Book Review* (do not have copy).

Nov. 19, 1968 - *National Review* article (do not have copy).

Nov. 1968: *Review* of *War and Peace in the Global Village* by Vincent Di Norcia entitled "The Sanity of Madness or McLuhan Re-vued" - *Laurentian Review,* Vol. 1, #2, pp. 132-39.

"Noble Purpose But to What End?" - *Chicago Tribune, Book World,* 11 (Nov. 10, 1968) p. 4.

"Marshall McLuhan" by Richard Kostelanetz - chapter in *Innovations* Ed. Bernard Bergonzi, published by Melbourne Toronto Press, 1968, pp. 134-149.

"The Soft Machine" by Thomas Edwards - *Partisan Review,* 35 (Summer 1968), p. 433.

"Media Crises" by Andrew Forge - *Studio International,* 175 (March 1968), p. 162. Review of *Medium is the Massage - Verbo-Voco Visual.*

"McLuhan Talks about McLuhanism" - Robt. Fulford - *Presbyterian Survey,* March, 1968.

"A Selective Bibliography of the Writing of and About Marshall McLuhan" by Toby Goldberg, in *Journal of Broadcasting,* 22 (Spring, 1968) 179.

"Hardware Store" - *Time,* 92 (August 9, 1968), p. 48.

"It's Time to Burn Off McLuhan" - Roy Higgins, *Television* (Feb. 1968), pp. 38-43.

Hot Theology in a Cool World" by Ralph E. James in *Theology Today,* XXIV (Jan. 1968), p. 432.

"Columbus of Communications" by Penny Jones - *Frontier,* 11 (Spring, 1968), p. 31.

"The Medium is the Massage" by John Kean - *Teachers College Record,* 69 (Jan. 1968), p. 400. Review of MM.

"McLuhan" by Marcia Keller - *Library Journal,* 43 (Dec. 15, 1968), 4742.

"McLuhan's Message Or: Which Way Did the Second Coming Went?" by Milton Klonsky - *New American Review,* No. 2 (Jan. 1968), p. 95.

"McLuhan, Hero or Heretic" by Harold B. Kuhn - *Christianity Today* 12 (Sept. 13, 1968) p. 8.

"The McLuhan Thesis: Its Limits and Its Appeal" by Edward Lueders, *English Journal,* 58 (April 1968), p. 565.

"Marketing the Message" - *Newsweek,* 72 (July 15, 1968), p. 54.

"Christian and McLuhan" by Raymer B. Matson - *Dialog,* 8 (Autumn, 1968), p. 259.

"What About McLuhan?" by Frank McElroy and Francis P. Jones - *Christian Century,* 85 (July 31, 1968), p. 973.

"McLuhan" - *Kirkus,* 36 (Sept. 1, 1968), 1021. *Review of War and Peace in the Global Village.*

"McLuhan: Cool Counsel" - *Newsweek,* 72 (Nov. 11, 1968), p. 27.

"McLuhan, Media and the Ministry" by Thos. J. Michael, *Christian Century,* 85 (May 29, 1968).

"Future as History . . . An Interpretation of Marshall McLuhan" - *Soundings,* 51 (Spring, 1968), p. 80. (by Albert Rabil Jr.)

"McLuhanism: The Natural History of an Intellectual Fashion" by Arnold Rockman in *Encounter,* 31 (Nov. 1968), p. 28.

"Cooling Down the Classroom: Some Educational Implications of the McLuhan Thesis" by Robert Sidwell in *Educational Forum* (March, 1968), p. 351.

"Understanding McLuhan: Some Implications for the Speech Teacher and Critic" by John H. Sloan in *Speech Teacher* 17 (March, 1968), p. 140.

"But What If McLuhan Is Right?" by DePaul Travers, in *Catholic World* 208 (June, 1968), p. 111.

"Understanding Media" - *Western World Review* 4 (Spring, 1968), p. 12. Review of *Und. Media.*

"The Charlatan as Saint" by Geoffrey Wagner in *National Review* 20 (Nov. 19, 1968, p. 1174. Review of *War and Peace in the Global Village, Through the Vanishing Point.*

"Aesthetics and Science" by Bary Wallenstein in *Catholic World,* 208 (Dec. 1968), p. 137. Review of *Through the Van. Pt.* and *From Cliche to Archetype.*

"Dichter on McLuhan" by Barbara Williams in *Twentieth Century* 177 (second Quarter 1968), p. 10.

"McLuhanism, Television, and Politics" by Edgar Willis in *Quat. J. Speech,* 54 (Dec. 1968), p. 404.

"McLuhan: Through Electric Circuitry to God" by Tom Wolfe in *Book World,* 2 (Sept. 15, 1968), p. 4. Review of *Through the Van. Point,* and *War and Peace in the Global Village.*

"Massaging McLuhan" by Paul D. Zimmerman in *Newsweek,* 72 (Sept. 23, 1968), p. 102. Review of *War and Peace in the Global Village.*

## 1969

Book    *Pour Comprendre MMcL* - published by the Association des Compagnons de Lure: Recontres 1969. Articles by G. Gheerbrant, R. Ponot, G. Blanchard, F. Richaudeau, M. Haumont, C. Corvisar, G. Lagneau et Fernand Baudin. Includes interview of McLuhan by G. Stearn translation by Fernand Baudin. (France)

"The Hardware/Software Mergers: How Successful Have They Been?" Reappraisal of the Educational Technology Industry - Proceedings of a conference held in November 16-18, 1969 at the Centre for Continuing Education, University of Chicago. Book published by Urban Research Corporation, Chicago. Prof. McLuhan's participation is on pages 1 to 39.

Thesis    Note received that Kathleen C. Barber completed her Master's thesis at the University of North Carolina on the subject of McLuhan as Historian. (Information received from Mrs. Barber's daughter, Kathleen Muller, 2419 Terrell Place, Lynchburg, Virginia, on Nov. 1, 1973).

Article in *Canadian Forum,* February, 1969 (do not have copy)

Article in *Sewanee Review,* Spring, 1969 (do not have copy).

"McLuhan vs. ad man TV debate is really off" - STAR, May 15, 1969. CBC had wanted to arrange debate between Prof. McLuhan and Jerry Goodis, advertising executive on program "The Way It Is." Mr. Goodis had previously received publicity in the STAR when he said: 'Menace' McLuhan can't communicate (we have copy of this article, but no date) and again on May 10, 1969 when he got a large writeup in the STAR by Harry Bruce entitled: "The ad man who claims McLuhan peddles only hogwash and hokum."

*Playboy* Interview: Marshall McLuhan - done by Eric Norden - Vol. 16, No. 3, March, 1969, pp. 53-158.

"What If He Is Right?" by Tom Wolfe - *The Pump House Gang* published by Bantam Books, N.Y. 1969, pp. 105-133.

*The Influence of Teilhard De Chardin and Marshall McLuhan,* by Richard Basil McCafferty - Ph.D., Northwestern University, 1969 (Abstract in Dissertation Abstracts, XXX, p. 3126-A).

*The Basis for Marshall McLuhan's Concepts of the Effects of Television Viewing* - by Frank W. Oglesbee, Ph.D., Univ. of Missouri, Columbia, 1969 (Abstract in Dissertation Abstracts, XXX, p. 3571-A).

"Imperialism and Irrationalism" by Herbert Aptheker in *Telos* IV (Fall, 1968), pp. 168-175.

"McLuhan: Pro and Con Man" by John Aden in Sewanee Review, 78 (Spring, 1969), p. 357.

"Recent Publications" by John Beach, in *Liturgical Arts,* 38 (Nov. 1969), p. 22.

"A Guide Through the Sensory Mazes" by Ralph Cohen in *Virginia Quarterly Review,* 45 (Winter, 1969), p. 162. Review of *Through the Van. Pt.*

Review of *War and Peace in the Global Village* by Peter Dart in *Journalism Quarterly,* 46 (Summer, 1969), p. 376.

"Fortune Cookie" by Dennis Duffy in *Nation,* 209 (Dec. 1969), p. 638.

"Marshall McLuhan: Educational Implications" by W.J. Gushue in *McGill Journal of Education,* 4 (Spring, 1969), p. 3.

"Browsing" by Gerald Kennedy in *Together,* 13 (Jan. 1969), p. 62. Review of *Through the Van. Pt.*

"Marshall McLuhan Interviewed" by Frank Kermode in *Month,* 228 (April, 1969), p. 219.

"McLuhan" - *Kirkus,* 37 (Sept. 1, 1969), p. 976. Review of *Interior Landscape.*

"Through the Vanishing Point" Review by Ross Mendes in *Canadian Forum,* 48 (Feb. 1969), p. 255.

"McLuhan: Pro and Con" by Allen J. Moore, in *Christian Advocate* XIII, (May 1, 1969), p. 17.

"Pour Comprendre McLuhan" by Edgar Morin, in *La Quinzaine Litteraire* (du 16 au 31 mars, 1969), pp. 69-74.

"Letter to *Playboy*" - *Playboy* (July 1969), p. 2.

"Playboy Interview" - Marshall McLuhan - *Playboy* 16 (Mar. 1969), 62.

"Back to the Future" by A. Perry in *Encounter,* 30 (Summer, 1969), p. 240.

"Apocalypse: The Medium is the Message" by Eugene H. Peterson, in *Theology Today,* 24 (July 1969), p. 133.

"Avant et Apres McLuhan" by Pierre Yves Petillion, in *Critique* 265 (June 1969), p. 504. Review of *Mechanical Bride.*

"War and Peace in the Global Village" a review by John Smee in *Sign,* 47 (Jan. 1969), p. 55.

"Message et Massage" by M. Souchon in *Etudes,* 330 (Jan. 1969), p. 141. Review of *Medium is the Massage.*

"Pour Comprendre Les Media" by M. Souchon in *Etudes* 330 (Feb. 1969), p. 393. Review of *Und. Media.*

"The Gutenberg Galaxy" by F.E. Sparshott in *Journal of Aesthetics and Art Criticism,* 3 (July 1969), p. 135. Review of *Through the Van. Pt.*

"This Week" - *Christian Century,* 84 (Dec. 3, 1969), p. 1552.

"McLuhan's Message Before he Discovered the Media" by Geoffrey Wagner, in *Book World,* 3 (Nov. 30, 1969), p. 15.

"The Four Gospels" by Michael Wood, in *New Society,* XIV (Dec. 18, 1969), p. 972.

"Why the Medium is a Mess: McLuhan and On-Air Recall Testing" by Matthew D. Chamlin - in Marketing Review, Vol. 25, #3, Nov. 1969 (published by the American Marketing Association, N.Y.) pp. 25-26.

"Lament for the media: what will become of us in the electronic age?" by Michael Barkway in The Financial Times of Canada, Dec. 22, 1969, a review of *Counterblast.*

"Le Message, c'est le Medium" in *Montreal-Matin,* Que., Aug. 20, 1969.

"Difficulties pour McLuhan" par Cy Fox in *Le Nouvellists, Que. December 1, 1969.*

"Holds Up Book" by Cy Fox in *Moncton Transcript,* N.B. Nov. 27, 1969. re *Counterblast.*

"Le Prophete McLuhan nous entrouvre les portes de l'an 1990" in *Chatelaine,* Montreal, Sept. 1969. Article by Fernande Saint-Martin. Review of *Mutations 1990.*

"Wild Book in Trouble Before It's Even Printed" by Cy Fox in *Red Deer* Advocate, Alta. Nov. 25, 1969 - re *Counterblast.*

"Publishing is Delayed" - Cy Fox in *Charlottetown Patriot,* P.E.I. Nov. 25, 1969. (re *Counterblast).*

Comment on *Counterblast* by Ron Grant (Book Editor) in *Montreal Gazette,* Que. Nov. 29, 1969.

"McLuhan's Book Stalled by Robbery" - Cy Fox in *Kitchener Waterloo Record,* Nov. 24, 1969. (re *Counterblast).*

"Blind faith loves neutral bias" review of *Counterblast* by Dennis Duffy in *The Globe & Mail,* Nov. 22, 1969.

"Blast McLuhan — Bless him, too" - review of *Counterblast* in *The Province,* Dec. 12, 1969.

"More of the rear-view mirror" - Review of *Counterblast* in *Prairie Messenger,* Sask. Dec. 21, 1969.

"The Medium is the Mess-age" by Bernie Harder in *The Canadian Mennonite,* Dec. 12/6, p. 7 - Review of *Counterblast.*

**1969-
1970**   "McLuhanism on the rampage is a real blast" by Norm Ibsen for the *London Evening Free Press,* Dec. 9, 1969. re *Counterblast.*

"Revised Standard Version" by William Morgan - review of *Counterblast* in *Winnipeg Free Press,* Jan. 17, 1970. p. 21.

*"The Concept of involvement in Marshall McLuhan"* - in ADMAP, Oct. 1969 by John Rowan - pp. 434 to 438.

*"The Four Gospels - Laing, Levi-Strauss, Lorenz and McLuhan"* by Michael Wood - in New Society, Dec. 18, 1969. pp. 972-975.

*Nuestro Tiempo* - Sept. 1969, No. 16, Vol. XXXII, #183 - booklet contains article by John W. Mole "La comunicacion: de Heraclito a McLuhan," p. 294-301.

Nov. 25, 1969 - Voice of the People section of the *Star* - Short piece entitled "Blast McLuhan."

Note rec. from James Milton Highsmith, Eng. Dept., San Francisco College for Women, Lone Mountain, San Francisco, 94118 stating he had just written a review of *Counterblast* and *The Interior Landscape* for the San Francisco Chronicle. He did not send copy of the review. (Dec. 6/69).

"Private Citizens Work to Find, Save Historic Sites" by Sue Hutchison Seattle Post-Intelligencer, Sun. Nov. 16, 1969. Quotes McLuhan.

"In Defense of Print-Heads" - article by Rex Lardner in *The New York Times Book Review,* Oct. 1969 mentions McLuhan.

"Experimental Investigation of McLuhan's Ideas Concerning Effects of "Hot" and "Cool" Communications Media" - article by Wolfgang G. Bringmann, Wm. D.G. Balance, Alan Krichev (Univ. of Windsor) appeared in Psychological Reports, 1969, 25, pp. 447-451. Study carried out to investigate theories of McLuhan. From a paper read at Southeastern Psychological Assoc. Meeting in New Orleans, Feb.-Mar. 1969.

Marshall mentioned on pages 1, 2 and 4 of Jim Atkins Newsletter on Communication (published by himself) - no date on this, but it was rec. in 1969.

Review of *The Interior Landscape* (McLuhan) written by D. Dooley for SMC Alumni Assoc. Newsletter, Spring, 1970.

"Mind of McLuhan" Letter to the Editor of the *Guardian,* England, by Michael Claxton, 5 Dryden Rd. Bush Hill Park, Enfield, Middlesex Sept. 1969 (no date given).

*Radical School Reform* edited by Ronald and Beatrice Gross (Simon and Schuster, New York) - 1969 - "The editors turn their attention to the theorists, Goodman, Dennison, Clark, McLuhan, etc.

*Marshall McLuhan* by Dennis Duffy, McClelland & Stewart, Toronto, 1969-1970.

"Marshall McLuhan's theories are a means to an end, not an end in themselves" review of Dennis Duffy's book on McLuhan by Tony Gifford in *Monday Morning* magazine, Jan./Feb. 1970 pp. 34-35.

## 1970

Thesis *An Explanation of the Perceptions of Marshall McLuhan as Indicated in his Major Works with a View to Discovering his Underlying Philosophy and its Educational and Sociological Implications* - by *Kamala Bhatia* - A dissertation submitted to the School of Graduate Studies, State University of New York at Buffalo, in partial fulfillment of the requirements for the Degree of Doctor of Philosophy - May, 1970.

Thesis *The Effect of Electronic Media on the Structure of Marketing Jerry Teitelbaum,* Thesis submitted in partial fulfillment of the requirements for the degree of Master of Business Administration, Bernard M. Baruch School of Business and Public Administration, the City College of the City University of New York, January 1970. (uses many quotes from McLuhan).

Thesis *A Comparative Analysis of Three Themes From the Existentialist Soren Kierkegaard with the Communication Theory of Marshall McLuhan* - John Francis Graham, Berkeley, California, Nov. 1970 A thesis submitted to the faculty of San Francisco State College in partial fulfillment of the requirements for the degree of Master of Arts.

Professor McLuhan written up in *Pears Cyclopedia* 79th edition Published by The Chaucer Press Ltd., 1970, Pelham Books Ltd. Notations on page B-50 and page J-26. (Letters should be addressed to: The Editor, "Middlemarch" Halstead, Sevenoaks, Kent, England.)

Manuscript *Revolution, Revolution, Counter-Revolution: A Probe Into Marshall McLuhan for the Linear Minded.* Unpublished manuscript from Dr. Joseph Martos (St. Anne Religious Education Center, Room A, 312 East Chestnut Street, Barrington, Illinois, 60010, USA) received November 30, 1973.

"Today Show Corrects McLuhan Flag Joke" article in *The Telegram* Sept. 21, 1970.

"Kansas City Show" - *Sunday Magazine,* Ivan Goldman, January 4, 1970, pp. 29-31 and 36-38.

"McLuhan's Theories on TV seem confirmed by research" by Lotta Dempsey in *Toronto Star,* June 27, 1970, p. 85. (re Herbert E. Krugman report on brain wave studies he conducted in May, 1970 which appeared to confirm Professor McLuhan's views about differences between print and TV media).

Dr. Herbert E. Krugman, manager of corporate public opinion research at General Electric Company, 570 Lexington Avenue, New York, N.Y. 10022, delivered a paper to the American Association for Public Opinion Research at their annual conference on "Brain Wave Measurements of Media Involvement" (relating to Prof. McLuhan's theories). His address was published in the Journal of Advertising Research, Vol. 11, #1. February, 1971 (published by the Advertising Research Foundation Inc).

"Marshall McLuhan fad appears to be fading" by Dennis Duffy in *Toronto Star,* Nov. 21, 1970, p. 67.

"Students Cheer the Media Man" by Lincoln Kaye in *San Francisco Chronicle* comments on Prof. McLuhan's visit to San Francisco Univ. - appeared on Monday, Oct. 19, 1970.

"Toronto considered the leader in school reform, American says" Neil Postman comments on McLuhan - *Star,* Oct. 8, 1970, p. 26.

"Attack on Photos" Letter to the editor of *Editor & Publisher* re McLuhan and photography from Jim Atkins, Washington, D.C., October 24, 1970.

"The Sounds of McLuhan" by Lynn Ludlow for *San Francisco Examiner* Oct. 19, 1970, p. 3. - comments on McLuhan visit to Univ. of San Francisco on Oct. 18th.

"The Medium is McLuhan" by Alec Reid from Dublin who came to the Centre to observe McLuhan. Article appeared in *Newsight,* Dublin April, 1970, issue. pp. 68-72.

"McLuhan Calls Work on Media Lonely" by Edward Cowan appeared in *The New York Times,* Oct. 5, 1970.

"BIPR Gold Medal Presented to McLuhan" - short article and picture of Prof. McLuhan receiving gold medal award by the British Institute of Public Relations for "outstanding work in the field of modern communications" appeared in *Ontario Bulletin* from Queen's Park, December 1970 issue.

"McLuhan, hurrah" editorial appeared in the *Star* on December 3, 1970.

TV vs. Print - Article on McLuhan appeared in *Newsweek*, Nov. 2, 1970, p. 40 under "Media" section - tells of Krugman experiment.

"Teacher dedicated to saving civilization" by Lotta Dempsey in *Star,* Feb. 2, 1970 - full page - Section 2, page 17 - two large pictures of McLuhan.

"Marshall McLuhan: City Planners Live in the 19th Century" by Tom Davey, in Canadian Consulting Engineer, May, 1970, p. 28-29.

"Nota Sobre McLuhan" by Armando Mora de Oliveira (Separata da Revista Discurso no. 1, editada pelo Departamento de Filosofia da Vaculdade de Filosofia, Letras e Ciencias Humanas da Universidade de Sao Paulo) Sao Paulo, 1970.

Book    *Metaphor: An Annotated Bibliography and History* by Warren A. Shibles, The Language Press, Box 342, Whitewater, Wisconsin, 53190. (contains comments on McLuhan's work).

"Marshall McLuhan: Medium & Man" - *The Milwaukee Public Library Reader and Calendar of Local Events* - written by Vivian Maddox Assistant City Librarian in charge of the Central Library, Milwaukee, Wisconsin. (Vol. 28, #35, Aug. 31, 1970).

Full-page cartoon of McLuhan on front of *The Globe and Mail* Magazine Section, Friday, Aug. 21, 1970 done by artist Franklin noting that Prof. McLuhan was to appear as guest on "The New Majority" TV show on Monday, Aug. 24/70.

"Marshall McLuhan: That's not your office, it's a cave" article in Montreal AIA DAILY, magazine (Assoc. of Industrial Advertisers) after address given by Prof. McLuhan to the AIA on June 15, 1970. Published by McGraw-Hill Publications Company. Page 2.

"Marshall McLuhan, Provocateur" Review of *Counterblast* by Jim Floody appeared in *South Bend Tribune,* South Bend Indiana, April 26, 1970.

"Occidente Vuelve a Primitivismo Tribal" by Mr. Fausto Fernandez Ponte appeared in *Excelsior,* a newspaper in Mexico. Mr. Ponte had interviewed Prof. McLuhan for this article. The interview was arranged through the Dept. of External Affairs in Ottawa.

"A Worshipful Visit to the Shrine of McLuhan" by Alexander Ross in *The Financial Post,* Wed., April 15, 1970 (do not have page number).

"People Seen Getting Survival Emotion from Bad News" - article by Stanley Watson appeared in *Reading Eagle* (newspaper), Reading, Pa. from press interview at Albright College where Prof. McLuhan gave a lecture. Appeared May 5, 1970.

"One Man's Impact on Author McLuhan" - *Counterblast* review by William Ready in The Spectator, Hamilton, Ontario on February 14, 1970.

"McLuhan Backs no-walls schools for teens who dislike regular ones" article in *Star,* Toronto, on April 1, 1970.

"McLuhan Doctrine" by Nancy Ross - article in *The Washington Post* - comments on Prof. McLuhan's address to National Religious Broadcasters at the Statler Hilton Hotel - Wed., January 28, 1970.

"Burning Would comic rebuke of expressway backers" by Kaspars Dzeguze in Globe & Mail, Oct. 16, 1970.

"Marshall McLuhan Revisited" by Tom Saunders in *Winnipeg Free Press* May 22, 1970.

"She likes McLuhan message" by Marina Craig - article on Dr. Kamala Bhatia and her comments on Prof. McLuhan, in *The Spectator,* Hamilton, Oct. 9, 1970, page 27.

Published
Paper    "Tele-Revelations of Marshall McLuhan" by V. Av-
eryanov published in *Voprosy Literatury* (Questions of
Literature), No. 7, 1970 in the U.S.S.R. (Copy of paper
was sent to Prof. McLuhan from the Department of
External Affairs in Ottawa on January 12, 1971).

Thesis   *Communication Theory in the Works of Marshall
McLuhan,* by James I. Costigan - Ph.D. Southern Il-
linois University, 1970. (Abstract in Dissertation
Abstracts, XXXI, p. 3681-A.

Thesis   *McLuhan: An Inquiry Into His Retribalization Theory* -
by William Kirk. Kilpatrick - Ph.D. Purdue University,
1970 (Abstract in Dissertation Abstracts, XXX, P.
5534-A).

Review of *Counterblast* by George Sanderson in *The
Antigonish Review* #1, Spring, 1970, pp. 124-130.

"More Probes in the Same Spot" by Ken Burke in *New
Republic* 157 (Feb. 7, 1970), p. 30. Review of *Counterblast.*

"Treatment in Kind" by Richard Cremmerer in *Christian Century,* 87 (Feb. 4, 1970), p. 146. Review of *Counterblast.*

Article by Keith Cushman in *Library Journal,* 45 (Feb.
1, 1970), p. 497.

"To Scientifico Nell' Umans" by Francs Fanizza in
*Giornale Critico della Filosofia Italians,* 1 (April-June,
1970), p. 271.

"From Cliche to Archetype" review by John Fowles, in
*Saturday Review,* 53 (Nov. 21, 1970), p. 32.

"Is the McLuhan Age, Here to Stay, Hear to Stay, Here
Two Stray?" *ad 1970,* 1 (April 26, 1970), 4-9.

"Wood and the Videotape" by Dennis Johnson in *Christianity Today* 14 (Sept. 25, 1970), p. 8.

"Communications" by Bill Katz in *Library Journal,* 45
(Feb. 1, 1970), p. 491.

"McLuhan's Cut-Out Culture" by Stuart W. Little in *Saturday Review,* 53 (May 9, 1970), p. 68. Review of *Culture is Our Business.*

"Ludwig Wittgenstein Und Das Problem Diner Philosophische Anthropologie by F.K. Mayr in *Tydschrift voon Filosofie,* 32, (June, 1970), p. 214.

"Liturgical Medium In An Electronic Age" by Chas. C. McDonald, in *Worship,* 46 (Jan. 1970), p. 27.

"McLuhan" - *Kirkus,* 38 (July 15, 1970), p. 786. Review of *From Cliche to Archetype.*

"McLuhan on Religion" - *Christianity Today,* 14 (Feb. 13, 1970), p. 34.

"Verbal Vaudeville" by Neil Millar in *Christian Science Monitor* (July 23, 1970), p. 7. Review of *From Cliche to Archetype* and *Culture Is Our Business.*

Review of *Counterblast* by Regina Minudri in *Library Journal,* 95 (April 15, 1970), p. 1664.

"McLuhan: Ice-Cold" by David Newton de Molina in *Critical Quarterly* 22 (Spring, 1970), p. 78.

"Communications" by Joseph Palmer in *Library Journal,* 45 (Sept. 1, 1970), p. 2797. Rev. of *Cliche to Archetype* and *Culture Is Our Business.*

"Structures in Art Media" by Marian Pauson in *Tulane Studies in Philosophy,* 9 (  1970), p. 65.

"The Linear Teacher and the Non-Linear McLuhan" by Hayden Smith in *Clearing House,* 45 (Oct. 1970), p. 126.

"McLuhan and the Future of Literature" by Rebecca West in *Books,* No. 1, (Autumn, 1970), p. 6.

"McLuhan: Maximum Built-in Obsolescence - by John Fowles, a review of *From Cliche to Archetype,* in *The Toronto Telegram,* Sat., Nov. 28, 1970, p. 29. (sketch of Prof. McLuhan by David Annesley).

*Modern Masters* - editor: Frank Kermode. This is a series first launched in January, 1970, on "men who have changed and are changing the life and thought of our age." McLuhan on list of books to be published, but we don't appear to have further data. (Fontana books, Britain). See *McLuhan* by J. Miller below.

"Initial Proposals for a Joint Science-Humanities McLuhan Project" Paper (draft) received from Vince Lackner on July 15, 1970.

"Marshall McLuhan conceives first film" by Zena Cherry -a *Globe and Mail,* July 30, 1970, p. W2.

"McLuhan's theories on TV seem confirmed by research" by Lotta Dempsey, Star, June 27, 1970 (re Krugman experiments). p. 85.

Two quotes by McLuhan in NEWS, Federal Communications Commission publication, Washington, D.C. 20554 released on Nov. 5, 1970 quotes are on pp. 22 and 48.

"Poet W.H. Auden a delight at seminar in Irish Studies" by Don Rubin - article on panel discussion which took place at the U of T on Feb. 10 - panel consisted of Bucky Fuller, Marshall McLuhan, actor Jack MacGowran and Auden. Article appeared on Feb. 11, p. 26, 1971.

Picture and comment about the above seminar appeared in the *St. Catharines (Canada) Standard,* Feb. 13, 1971.

"McLuhan's Message" by Michael Linderman appeared in *Chicago Sun-Times* April 12, 1971, p. 66.

"McLuhan Out?" by Tim Devlin, (The *Times* of London) appeared in the *Globe & Mail,* April 2, 1971, p. 25.

*The Velluminous Word* by Richard Wasson - booklet published by University of Illinois, Urbana, Illinois, June, 1971. (contains various quotes from Und. Media and Gut. Galaxy).

"McLuhan hot new group" by Wayne Crawford in *Chicago Daily News,* Feb. 3, 1971 - article about six-man band calling themselves "McLuhan."

"Tele-Revelations of Marshall McLuhan" by V. Averyanov appeared in *Voprosy Literatury* (No. 7, 1970). Averyanov, a Soviet scholar, analyses the ideological essence of the view of Marshall McLuhan. (Voprosy Literatury - *Questions of Literature* - was published in the Soviet Union. Draft of article sent to Prof. McLuhan by J.G.H. Halstead, European Division, Dept. of External Affairs, Ottawa).

"Marshall McLuhan — What're ya doin'?" by Barry Callaghan in the Telegram, Feb. 27, 1971. (sketch of McLuhan also).

"Writer calls McLuhan a nostalgic reactionary" by Peter Sypnowich in the Star, Feb. 25, 1971 (re Jonathan Miller book on McLuhan).

**ook** *McLuhan* by Jonathan Miller, Fontana books, 139 pages, 1971. (and Viking Press, N.Y.).

**1971** Article by Henry Beissel, Assoc. Professor of English, Sir George Williams Univ. in the Star, April 5, 1971 "Sham 'verities' of the anti-nationalists" mentions McLuhan.

"Man and Media in the Electronic Phase of Civilization" by Peter Pribyl in *Hospodarske Noviny,* Prava 4, Czechoslovakia, Feb. 1971. Review of *Counterblast.*

"McLuhan: A Progress Report" by Tom Mancuso in *Fusion* (New England Scene Publications Inc., 909 Beacon St., Boston, Mass.). pp. 22-24, Sept. 17, 1971.

Full page ad in *The New York Times,* on Tuesday, Aug. 24, 1971 — picture and comments. Top headline: "A criticism of television news from someone who knows, for a change."

"Different News Media" editorial in *Chicago-Tribune,* Aug. 29, 1971.

"McLuhan on Jewish PR Strategy" by Wilma Morrison in *The Canadian* Jewish News, Friday, Mar. 12, 1971, p. 3. (an interview).

"If only McLuhan did not rumble like a dinosaur" David Rowbotham's review of *Counterblast, The Medium is the Massage* and *Und. Media* in *Courier-Mail* Saturday Magazine (newspaper) Brisbane, Australia.

"Books and Marshall McLuhan" by Sam Neill in *The Library Quarterly*, Vol. #4, Oct. 1971, University of Chicago Press.

"With friends like this, McLuhan needs no enemies" Books section review of *The Medium is the Rear View Mirror* by Donald F. Theall. Several copies of this in file, but no indication of where it appeared or by whom.

Book *The Medium is the Rear View Mirror* by Donald F. Theall, McGill-Queen's Univ. Press, 1971.

"Do you really need to go to work today?" by Alexander Ross in the *Star,* Dec. 21, 1971.

"McLuhan: The Medium is the Message" by Chas. F. Hoban, Annenberg School of Communications, the Univ. of Pennsylvania. Publication issued by the ERIC Clearinghouse on Media and Technology, Stanford, Calif. 94305 in Sept. 1971. Article on pages 13-18.

"The troubled years: Claude Bissell looks back" in *Globe & Mail* Mar. 22, 1971 - Prof. Claude Bissell remarks about Prof. McLuhan in this article.

"We Have Met the Sassenachs and They Are Ours: Even the Year is Now McMLXIX" - poem about Marshall McLuhan by Ogden Nash - no info. about where this was published, or the year. Original in 1971 file of "Articles About."

Thesis *An Examination of the Evolution of Jazz as it Relates to Pre-Literate, Literate and Post-Literate Percepts of Marshall McLuhan* - James J. Quinn - Northwestern University - A Dissertation submitted to the Graduate School in Partial Fulfillment of the requirements for the degree of Doctor of Philosophy, Field of Speech, June, 1971. (Evanston, Illinois).

esis    *Marshall McLuhan's Social and Educational Ideas* -
Ernest P. Carriere A Dissertation presented to the
Faculty of the Graduate College in the University of
Nebraska in partial fulfillment of requirement for the
Degree of Doctor of Education, Dept. of History and
Philosophy of Education, Lincoln, Nebraska, June,
1971.

esis    *Some Selected Aphrisms of Marshall McLuhan and
Their Implications for High School Teaching* - Judith
Smith Busse - A Thesis presented to the Graduate
Council of The University of Tennessee in partial ful-
fillment of the requirements for the Degree Master of
Science, June, 1971.

*A Probe Into Marshall McLuhan for the Linear-minded* -
Joseph Martos Unpublished paper submitted to Prof.
McLuhan on May 21, 1971 by Mr. Martos, 1005 Cres-
cent Parkway, Fox River Grove, Illinois, 60010.

"Understanding Media: McLuhan in the Ontario
Classroom" - presentation to the Canadian Council of
Teachers of English conference held at McGill Univer-
sity Aug. 18 to Aug. 21, 1971 by John Atkin.

"Marshall McLuhan and Education" A Presentation by
Dr. Ross Hall Chairman, Dept. of Biochemistry,
McMaster University in Physical Sciences Bldg. Room
17, March 17, 1971 at 7:30 p.m.

"Seminar on Marshall McLuhan" by Dr. K. Bhatia at
McMaster University School of Adult Education on
Tues., May 4, 1971 at 7:30 p.m.

"Marshall McLuhan and Harold Innis" Presentation by
Dean R.R. Jamieson, of Mohawk College of Applied
Arts and Technology, McMaster University, March 24,
1971 at 7:30 p.m.

"Books and Marshall McLuhan" Paper by Sam Neill,
Associate Professor, School of Library and Information
Science, University of Western Ontario (unpublished
paper).

"Inquest on McLuhan" by George Woodcock - *The Nation,* Nov. 1, 1971, p. 437.

**Thesis** *An Examination, Critique and Evaluation of the Mass Communications Theories of Marshall McLuhan* - Ph.D. - University of Wisconsin, 1971 by Toby Goldberg. (Abstract in Dissertation Abstracts, XXX, p. 2112-A).

In *The Antigonish Review* #7, Autumn, 1971, George Sanderson did several pages on what he called X-O-TICS - on page 53 he did an "X-O-TIC" on "the medium is the message" which he calls "one of the briefest expositions of Dr. McLuhan's thought in the world."

"Christopher Booker on McLuhan" - Chris. Booker, in *Spectator,* 224 (Jan. 30, 1971), p. 160.

"Just the Tellings Man" by W. Booth in *Christian Reader* (Oct.-Nov., 1971), p. 58.

"Out of Orbit" by Neil Compton in *Canadian Literature,* 47 (Winter, 1971), 91. Review of *Counterblast* and *Interior Landscape.*

"Science and Profession" by G.P. Eliott in his *Conversions Literature and the Modernist Deviation,* 1971, p. 36.

"Unified English, Salvaging the Disaffected" by Edward Fagan in *Clearing House,* 45 (Jan. 1971), p. 259.

"More and Tyndale's Controversy Over Revelation" by James Hitchcock in *Journal of the American Academy of Religion,* 39 (Dec. 1971), p. 448.

"Culture Is Our Business" review by Thos. Lay in *Review for Religion* 30 (Jan. 1971), p. 155. Review of *Culture Is Our Business.*

"The Cartesian Constellation" by Joseph Martos in *Kinesis: Graduate Journal in Philosophy,* 3 (Spring 1971), p. 63.

"Metarhetorics of Plato, Augustine, and McLuhan" by James J. Murphy in *Philosophy and Rhetoric,* 4 (Fa. 1971), p. 201.

Review of *From Cliche to Archetype* by John J. Murray in *Best Sellers,* 30 (Jan. 1, 1971), p. 424.

"Theories of Social Change and the Mass Media" by John Palmer in *Journal of Aesthetic Education,* 5 (Oct. 1971), p. 127.

"Fossilized Socialist, Soured Enthusiast" by Raymond Rosenthal in *New Leader,* 54 (May 17, 1971), p. 24.

"McLuhan's Something" by Alan Ryan in *Listener,* 85 (Jan. 14, 1971), p. 55.

"McLuhan" by M. Souchon in *Etudes,* 334 (Mar. 1971), p. 470.

"It's McLuhan, But Is It New?" by Alan Wingard in *The Charlotte Observer* January 10, 1971 - Review of *From Cliche to Archetype.* (North Carolina), p. 5B.

*The Great Canadian Novel* by Harry Boyle (Doubleday, 1972). Marshall is mentioned on two pages in this book. (Eric).

Large article in Israeli newspaper - interview was done by Dr. Aberhami who came to Centre - article appeared on June 30, 1972.

"The Doctrine of Mass Media According to the Revelations of Marshall McLuhan" - paper read by Bob Scott at the University of Hawaii on April 10, 1972 when Prof. McLuhan was lecturing there.

"Look to Retirement with Anticipation" in *Topical* Published by the Civil Service Commission, Toronto, November 10, 1972, 4/19 after Prof. McLuhan gave talk to group when it launched its pilot course for pre-retirment education for civil servants.

Clipping from Lisbon newspaper sent in by Robt. Kilpatrick of Longmans Canada Ltd. with writeup on Prof. McLuhan and his picture. We do not have any details on this.

"Marshall McLuhan and French Structuralism" by James M. Curtis in *Boundary 2,* Suny-Binghamton, New York, Fall, 1972.

"McLuhan-Per Anik ad Astra?" in *Radio Canada International* No. 1, Spring, 1973. (C.P. 6000, Montreal, Canada), Program Schedule Bulletin.

"McLuhan's Media Charts Related to the Process of Communication" by Sam Neill, Assoc. Professor, School of Library and Information Science, Univ. of Western Ontario. (unpublished), Draft rec. January 4, 1973.

"Writing in Canada: Innis, McLuhan and Frye: Frontiers of Canadian Criticism" by Jon Slan in *Canadian Dimension*, October, 1972.

"Sharing the News - Friendly Teamness: Teeming Friendness" Booklet published in 1971 by ABC Owned Television Stations division for the purpose of presenting the observations of Professor McLuhan.

*McLuhan: a pocketful of mirrors* by Mark Slade, published by the National Film Board of Canada, Vol. V, #3, 1972.

*A Theological Critique of Marshall McLuhan's New Man of the Electric Age* Dissertation presented to the Faculty of the School of Theology in partial fulfillment of the requirements for the Degree of Doctor of Philosophy in Theology, Aquinas Institute of Philosophy and Theology, Dubuque, Iowa, 1972, by Allen Maruyama.

"Review of *From Cliche to Archetype* by D.C. Williams in *University of Toronto Quarterly*, 41 (Summer 1972), p. 413.

"The Pop Intellectual as Antichrist" by Henry Winthrop in *Journal of Aesthetics and Art Criticism*, 6 (Jan.-Apr. 1972), p. 211.

"Inquest on McLuhan" by George Woodcock in *Nation*, 213 (Nov. 1, 1971), p. 437

"Don't dare stop in moving world" - a review of *Take Today: The Executive as Dropout* (McLuhan and Nevitt) by Maureen Peterson in *The Expositor*, Brantford, Sat., Dec. 9, 1972, p. 6.

"The User is the Content" review of *Take Today: The Executive as Dropout* by Bent Stidsen, (Asst. Professor of Marketing, McMaster University, Hamilton, Ont.) in *Books,* Sept. 18, 1972, pp. 53-55 (with caricature by Pilsworth).

Write-up about *Take Today* in *Shop* (The National Newspaper of Used and Surplus Equipment, Toronto, Ont.), October, 1972.

"Coping with 'magnetic city'" review of *Take Today* by Joseph P. Larkin in *National Catholic Reporter,* August 18, 1972, p. 14.

"Message, Message, Who's Got the Message?" by Ralph Novak for Newspaper Enterprise Association/New York-Cleveland May 25, 1972 about his interview with Prof. McLuhan and Barrington Nevitt about their new book *Take Today: The Executive as Dropout.*

"With McLuhan, You Listen" a write-up about *Take Today* in *Herald Magazine,* Thurs., June 29, 1972, page 6.

"McLuhan on those who idolize him: 'Immature semi-literates'" by Kildare Dobbs in *The Toronto Star,* Sat., July 8, 1972, reviewing *Take Today,* page 67.

"An Enchanting Book — and a Pile of Rubbish" by E.D. Ward-Harris - a review of *Take Today* in *The Daily Colonist,* (Eng.), Sun., July 23, 1972, p. 15.

"McLuhan massages his medium" by Hendrik Overduin - a review of *Take Today* in *The Windsor Star,* Sat., Aug. 19, 1972, p. 38.

"Newed Figours Apun Marshy Grownd" by Leo Simpson - a review of *Take Today* in *Books in Canada,* August, 1972, p. 6-7.

*Take Today: The Executive as Dropout* - a review by Anthony Barton in *Quill and Quire,* Toronto, Ont. June, 1972.

"McLuhan tosses out old room-at-the-top thinking" by Arnold Edinborough - a review of *Take Today* in *Financial Post,* July 1, 1972, page 7.

In her column 'After a Fashion' in the *Globe and Mail*, July 6, 1972 Zena Cherry mentions *Take Today* by Marshall McLuhan and Barrington Nevitt.

"Mind Expanding" by R.C. Malone - a review of *Take Today* in *Winnipeg Free Press,* Friday, June 30, 1972 - *Books* section, page 21, done by R.C. Malone.

"Does the future belong to the *software* operators? - by Mark W. Weber in *Showcase/Chicago Sun Times,* Sun., June 18, 1972, page 19. A review of *Take Today.*

"McLuhan dissects the executive" - a review of *Take Today* in *Business Week,* June 24, 1972, p. 118.

**Thesis** *The Effect of Marshall McLuhan's Concept of Perception on the Oral* Interpretation of Literature - Jack Calvin Kingsley University of California, Los Angeles - A dissertation submitted in partial satisfaction of the requirements for the Degree of Doctor of Philosophy in Speech, 1972.

Professor Joel Persky, Lecturer in Mass Communications, Herbert H. Lehman College of the City University of New York, Dept. of Speech and Theatre, teaching course on "Marshall McLuhan's Theories of Mass Communications" during 1973 semester.

*Marshall McLuhan in the Magic Kingdom: From the Ear to the Eye* Paper written by A. Gordon Murray, presented at a Conference on Educational Development in Nepal. Copy of paper sent to Professor McLuhan Sept. 6, 1972.

**Thesis** *The McLuhan Thesis and its Relationship to Contemporary Christian Apologetics* by William J. Fritts - Southwestern Baptist Theological Seminary in Fort Worth, Texas. (Advised Prof. McLuhan of his work in a letter, March 14, 1972).

**Thesis** *The Greek Character and Television in Greece* by Demetrios M. Gemelos. Thesis presented to The Department of Speech and Theater, Brooklyn College of the City University of New York in partial fulfillment of the requirements for the Degree of Master of Science, June, 1972. (Acknowledgements: Author expresses his appreciation to Dr. Marshall McLuhan whose concepts have guided the course of this study).

*Media and Communication* by Denis Diniacopoulos - copyright 1972 (P.O. Box 116, Montreal, 260, Que.). Mr. Diniacopoulos notes: "This book is written to be read by my students at the same time that they have to read Marshall McLuhan's *Understanding Media* which represents an exhaustive survey of media and their effects on man."

"En Route with McLuhan, Omnibus to the Magnetic City" by Peter Henniker-Heaton, *Christian Science Monitor*, May 17, 1972, p. 13. Review of *Take Today: The Executive as Dropout*.

"The Professor Bet" by R.M. Henderson - *Los Angeles Times*, March 6, 1972, Sec. 11, p. 6.

"McLuhan Delivers His Media Message" by Bella Stumbo - *Los Angeles Times*, Feb. 28, 1972, Section IV.

*Verbi-Voco-Visual Explorations in the Electric Age: A Study of Perception in the Writings of H. Marshall McLuhan* — Leo J. McKenzie - The Pontifical University of Saint Thomas Aquinas, Rome, 1972. A Dissertation submitted to the Philosophy Department in partial fulfillment of the requirements for the degree of Doctor of Philosophy.

*McLuhan's Conception of Post-Literacy: An Empirical Test* - P.R. *Lorion*, University of California, Los Angeles, 1972 - Ph.D. Sociology, general. (copies available from University Microfilms, A XEROX Company, Ann Arbor, Michigan).

Review of Jonathan Miller's *McLuhan* by George Sanderson in *The Antigonish Review* #9, Spring, 1972. (St. Francis Xavier University, Antigonish, Nova Scotia), pp. 105-6.

*Pour Comprendre Les Media - McLuhan* - by Francis Balle - published by Hatier, Paris, France, 1972. (paperback).

Mention of Prof. McLuhan made in "The Media and Social Change" by Richard K. Manoff - small booklet published for the 1972 Annual Meeting of Planned Parenthood Federation of America Inc. in San Antonio, Texas, Oct. 23, 1972.

"McLuhanism: A Message that Muddles" by Richard Gambino, in *Midwest Quarterly,* 14 (Oct. 1972, p. 53.

"Coping With the Magnetic City" by Joseph P. Larkin in *National Catholic Reporter,* 8 (Aug. 18, 1972), p. 14. Review of *Take Today.*

"McLuhan" by Daniel LaRosa in *Library Journal,* 47 (Mar. 15, 1972), p. 1030. Review of *Take Today.*

Review of *Take Today* by Robt. D. Nordbery in *Best Sellers,* 32 (June 1, 1972), p. 121.

"Pop Goes the Prophet" by Roderick Nordell in *Christian Science Monitor,* (Nov. 22, 1967), p. 17.

"Figuring the Ground: Notes on Some Theoretical Problems . . ." by F.E. Sparshott in *Journal of Aesthetic Education,* 6 (July 1972), p. 11.

"McLuhan and the Politics of Modernism" by Rich. Wasson in *Massachusetts Review,* 13 (Autumn, 1972), p. 567.

"Hoopla For the Future" by Reed Whittmore in *New Republic,* 164 (June 10, 1972), p. 27. Review of *Take Today.*

"More and Tyndale's Controversy Over Relevation: A Test of the McLuhan Hypothesis" - in the *Journal of the American Academy of Religion,* Vol. XXXIX, #4, December 1971, written by James Hitchcock, pp. 448 to 466.

"Nixon Won Our Election: McLuhan" - by Dalton Camp in *Star,* Nov. 20, 1972 - (picture of McLuhan).

"The Prophet of the Electric Age" by Rebecca Rass, in the *San Francisco Examiner & Chronicle* Aug. 20, 1972.

*Univ. of Western Ontario News* Bulletin - Vol. 8, #12, Sept. 28, 1972. Picture and writeup about Prof. McLuhan's honorary Doctor of Letters Degree which he is shown receiving from Chancellor John P. Robarts.

"Tuning in on Marshall McLuhan" by Joseph Foyle for special issue of *This Week,* Dublin, Ireland, in July, 1972. Professor McLuhan was a guest of Mr. Foyle when he went to Ireland to give a lecture at RDS Hall, Ballsbridge, Dublin. (pp. 23-26).

"After a Fashion: Honours for 5 gentlemen" by Zena Cherry in *Globe and Mail,* May 22, 1972 (re annual awards dinner where Prof. McLuhan was honoured at the Univ. of Detroit).

"McLuhan Delivers His Media Message" by Bella Stumbo re press conference with Prof. McLuhan at UCLA on Feb. 25 - article appeared in the *Los Angeles Times,* Monday, Feb. 28, 1972.

"McLuhan: Lots of Answers" by Watt Pye in *Register,* May 4, 1972.

"McLuhan brings 'Instant Future' to Colorado" by H.W. Scarborough re Prof. McLuhan's talk at Regis College on April 25-27/72 clipping sent, bqt no data.

"McLuhanisms Spark Parley" by Steve Johnston, also re Prof. McLuhan's talk at Regis College sponsored by the Denver Institute of Religion and Culture, appeared in the *Denver Post* on Apr. 26.

"Marshall McLuhan's Message" by Bella Stumbo in *International Herald Tribune,* Friday, March 3, 1972.

"Media-surfeited man said turning to occult" - heading of article in The London Free Press, Sept. 22, 1972 - article covers convocation ceremony at the Univ. of Western Ontario on Sept. 21 when Prof. McLuhan received an honorary degree. (picture of Prof. McLuhan).

"Through a Shutter Brightly: Notes on the New Composition" by Bruce A. Lohof - in The Centennial Review (publisher not shown, or date, on Xeroxed copy of article sent here by Prof. Marshall Fishwick).

"De P.R. - man in MacLuhans superkolossale schouwspel" article by J.P.M. van Santen appeared in *Provisorium* Aug.-Sept. 1972, No. 8, Holland. Includes picture of Van Santen & Prof. McLuhan at Sutton Place hotel.

**1973** *Marshall McLuhan: an interview with Jean Pare* - *Forces* magazine No. 22, 1973 - published by Hydro Quebec, pp. 5-25.

*La Publicidad, Profesion Intelectual,* by Eulalio Ferrer Rodriquez, Presidente, Publicidad Ferrer, S.A. (Miquel Angel De Quevedo No. 8, Mexico 20, D.F.). Frequent references to Prof. McLuhan in this book.

"Communicating" by Harry Bruce, *Globe & Mail,* Apr. 19, 1973, makes reference to Prof. McLuhan.

"McLuhan predicts 'electric liturgy' on worldwide TV' in *Star* June 2, 1973 (picture).

"Two graduations for fall '72" *Alumni Gazette,* The University of Western Ontario, Spring 1973, Vol. XLIX, #2, page 17. (re convocation - two degrees - Dr. Wilder G. Penfield and Marshall McLuhan).

*Ad* in *World Magazine.* 1973 - "Marshall McLuhan says the printed word is obsolete. To prove it, he wrote fifteen books." (copy in file). Copy of this ad appeared in *Saturday Review of The Arts,* April, 1973, Vol. 1, #4, page 10.

"Watergate - participatory torture, says McLuhan" - Campus magazine Oct./Nov. 1973, Vol. 6, #3, p. 3-4. (re Prof. McLuhan's address at Osgoode Hall Law School on October 17).

*Baroque and Aquarius: Two Poetic Sequences linked by Pictor Ignotus' Letter to McLuhan* - Paper (74 pages - prob. unpublished), received from Timothy Suttor, Religious Studies, University of Windsor, Feb. 13, 1973.

*Classical and Contemporary Rhetoric: The Theories of Aristotle and Marshall McLuhan* - Paper written by Karen Jacobson, sophomore government and politics major at the University of Maryland for Western Literature course. Copy of paper received Dec. 3, 1973.

"McLuhan to Untangle Watergate" article by Helen Worthington re Prof. McLuhan's upcoming talk at Senaca College on August 24. Article appeared in the *Star* on July 23, 1973.

"The Mythos of the Electronic Revolution" by James W. Carey and John J. Quirk in Spring 170 issue of the *Scholar*. Prof. Carey is director of the Institute of Communications research at the University of Illinois.

*Vie Des Arts* (magazine), Vol. XVIII, #72, Autumn, 1973, pp. 13-23. Articles by Don Theall and Derrick DeKerckhove (360, rue McGill, Montreal 125, Canada).

*Media and Meaning: Human Expression and Technology* - Series on the Media - scripts and slides - published by The Center for Humanities Inc., Two Holland Avenue, White Plains, New York 10603 - (Xerox copy of pages from the series are all that we have here). Professor McLuhan is quoted throughout the series. Xeroxed pages received Dec. 18, 1973.

"Avon Reissuing Seven Hoffenberg Novels" by Wm. S. Murphy - *Los Angeles Times,* February 25, 1973, Section Books, 13.

"McLuhan Calls Objectivity Old-Fashioned" - *Washington Post,* May 27, 1973, Section F-15.

"Sports Culture Scores Hollow Victories" article by George B. Leonard in *Rochester Democrat and Chronicle,* Sunday, Sept. 30, 1973, features picture of Prof. McLuhan with caption: "McLuhan: Competition creates resemblance."

"Misunderstanding McLuhan" by Richard Schickel in *More* magazine, N.Y. August, 1973, pp. 10-11 and 14-15. Appeared in the Toronto *Globe and Mail* on August 31, 1973 on p. 7 retitled "In canonizing McLuhan media missed the message" (excerpts).

"Leo Etudes Sociales" by Jean Bonefant, in *University of Toronto Quarterly,* 42 (Summer 1973), p. 475.

"McLuhancy: Counter-Rev in Cultural Theory" by John Fekete in *Telos,* 8 (Spring, 1973), p. 75.

"Human Behavior in Organizations" - *Library Journal,* 98 (March 1, 1973), p. 710.

"McLuhan's Media Charts Related to the Process of Communication" by S.D. Neill in *AV Communication* 21 (Fall 1973), p. 277.

Review of *Take Today* by Sam Neill in *Library Quarterly,* 42 (April 1973), p. 170.

"Advertising is: making someone ill, then selling the cure" by John Slinger in *Globe and Mail,* Aug. 5, 1973, p. 5, noting comments made by Prof. McLuhan during conference on Integrity in Communication which took place at Seneca College Aug. 2-4/73.

**1974** *The Philosophical and Sociological Foundations of Education* - book by Bhatia and Bhatia, published by Doaba House, Delhi, March, 1974. Chapter in book on "The Educational Philosophy of Marshall McLuhan" (book is also available from Media and Educational Research Centre - Mrs. Kamala Bhatia, 23 Clifford St., Hamilton, Ont.).

Chapter in Book

"Four Post-Moderns: Four Catholics" article by Michael Schwartz appeared in two parts in Triumph magazine (278 Broadview, Warrenton, Pa. 22186, editor: Michael Lawrence) *Part 1:* Vol. 8, #3, March, 1974. *Part 2:* Vol. 9, #4, 1974, pp. 26-29.

"Raped by the TV-programme?" by Peter Noever after interview with Professor McLuhan appeared in *Die Presse* in Vienna, Austria, page 5, April 28, 1974.

"Effect on Instructional Television on Personality Perception" by Milton James McMenamin in *AVCR,* Vol. 22, #1, Spring, 1974, pp. 51-62. (*AVCR,* - Audiovisual Communication Review).

"Marshall McLuhan et l'energie du banal" by Gilles Marcotte in *Le Devoir* (Paris newspaper) June 15, 1974, p. 17.

"Entretien Avec . . . MARSHALL McLUHAN - Un mouvement invisible et spontane prend en charge la qualite de la vie" in *Le Monde* (Paris newspaper) page 1, May 31, 1974. (re publication of French edition of *From Cliche to Archetype*.

"Mediaprofeten McLuhan pa besok i Stockholm: "Jag vantar inte att folk ska forsta vad jag sager" - article in *Expressen* (newspaper) (page 19), in Stockholm, Sweden, on June 5, 1974 when Prof. McLuhan addressed the EBAV (Esselte-Bonnier-Audio-Visual) conference attended by 500 media executives from northern Europe. During the visit, Prof. and Mrs. McLuhan were guests of King Carl Gustaf XVI at a private luncheon.

"MacLuhan Parle De Giscard Etdes Femmes" in *Paris Match* magazine, Paris, France, p. 77, June 15, 1974.

Full page ad in *Le Monde,* Paris newspaper, May 8, 1974, p. 7 by "La Presse Quotidienne Regionale" entitled "La Response de Gutenberg a MacLuhan."

"Marshall McLuhan Still Doin' His Thing (Whatever It Is)" in *The Sunday Denver Post,* June 30, 1974, p. 25. "Marshall MacLuhan, prophete de la communication — II met en garde — "Attention — le dialogue ou la mort" - appeared in *Argus de la Presse,* Paris, France, July 22, 1974, pp. 39-43.

Letter to the Editor of the Toronto *Star* by Ev Munro in reply to the articlz by Henry Morgan published in the *Star* on Sept. 27, 1974.

*THE TV DRAMA AND THE DRAMA OF TV* by Professor Boris Grabnar, Gornji trg 15, 61000 Ljubljana, Yugoslavia. (He will send copy of the book to Professor McLuhan). Professor Grabnar is working on his next book which will be an extensive comparison "about Marx's and McLuhan's theories."

"McLuhan Parle De Giscard Etdes Femmes" in PARIS MATCH magazine, Paris, France, June 15, 1974, p. 77.

"Post-Mortem on McLuhan: A Public Figure's Emergence and Decline as Seen in Popular Magazines" by Everette E. Dennis in *Mass Comm Review,* Vol. 1, #2, April 1974, pp. 31-40 published by Temple University, Philadelphia, Pa. 19122.

Full page ad in LE MONDE, Paris, France, May 8, 1974, p. 7 by "La Presse Quotidienne Regionale" entitled "La response de Gutenberg a McLuhan."

"Marshall McLuhan Still Doin' His Thing (Whatever It Is)" in *The Sunday Denver Post,* June 30, 1974, p. 25.

"Marshall McLuhan, prophete de la communication — II met en garde — Attention — le dialogue ou la mort" - ARGUS de la PRESSE, Paris, July 22, 1974, pp. 39-43.

Paper     "McLuhan and Classification" by S.D. Neill, Associate Professor School of Library and Information Science, University of Western Ontario, for presentation at a Classification Conference in Bombay in January, 1975.

Thesis     "Mass Consciousness Meets Man: A Comparison of the Analytic Theory of Carl G. Jung and the Communications Theory of Marshall McLuhan" by Alex E. Brazynetz - submitted in fulfillment of the requirements for the Social and Behavioral Science Department, St. Mary Seminary, 1227 Ansel Road, Cleveland, Ohio, 44108 - September 3, 1974.

Mention made of Professor McLuhan on pages 8, 68, 149, 168, 189 of *A History of Underground Comics* by Mark James Estren (Straight Arrow Books, 625 Third St., San Francisco, Calif. 94107, 1974.

Professor McLuhan's work noted in "Designer, Design Process and Built Form: A Study of Design" - *Thesis* by Daniel Bruce Perry for Master of Architecture Degree, Univ. of Toronto, 1974, pp. 319-22.

Under "Cultural Crossroads" column in *Hibernia* (newspaper) Ireland - John Kelleher writes about "Marshall McLuhan, prophet of the television age," on Friday, July 19, 1974, p. 9.

"Puzzling out McLuhan" - letter to the editor of the *Star* re Professor McLuhan by William Ruddock, Toronto, in which he includes a limerick about McLuhan. January 8, 1974.

"Marshall McLuhan - Un mouvement invisible et spontane prend en charge la qualite de la vie" by Pierre Dommergues in *Le Monde* Paris newspaper, May 31, 1974, p. 1.

Mention made of Professor McLuhan in *Halfway Up Parnassus* by Claude Bissell. Book published by University of Toronto Press, 1974. pp. 38, 82 and 186.

"Multi-Media" by Herb Karl - A review of *Making Contact* - a series of six paperbacks published by Harcourt, Brace, Jovanovich Inc. N.Y. 1974. Interview with Prof. McLuhan appears in paperback entitled *Electric Media*. Review by Herb Karl in *English Journal*, Vol. 63, #7, Oct. 1974, pp. 121-122.

*12 T y p o Graphical Interpretations* by Willi Kunz - Book No. 16 in an edition of 36 - printed in Switzerland, 1973-74. (based on Professor McLuhan's work).

"A McLuhan is a McLuhan is a McLuhan" by Henry Morgan in *Toronto Star* article, Friday, Sept. 27, 1974, p. B6.

Review of *War and Peace in the Global Village* by Vincent DiNorcia entitled "The Sanity of Madness: McLuhan Re-Vued" in *Laurentian* Review, Univ. of Sudbury, 1968, pp. 133-139.

"TV, "Como una Droga Electronica," Dijo McLuhan" article in EXCELSIOR (newspaper) by Raul Torres Barron, Oct. 25, 1974, pages 1 and 13-A (with photo), Acapulco. (Prof. McLuhan was guest speaker at conference "Encuentro on Communication" in Acapulco on October 25, 1974).

Professor McLuhan mentioned in Zena Cherry's column in the *Globe and Mail* on November 7, 1974 re his trip to Acapulco on Oct. 23-27/74.

An interview by June Callwood in the *Globe and Mail*, Toronto, November 25, 1974.

Write-up in *University of Toronto Bulletin* about "The Club of GNU" *Futurists look ahead and behind*. Mention made of Professor McLuhan's participation in the conference on November 11, 1974.

*McLuhan et la Politique: Memoire de D.E.S. de Science Politique* by Jean Mercier, published by Universite de Paris 1, Department de Science Politique, January, 1975.

Write-up about Professor McLuhan's trip to Acapulco appeared in *Imagenes de Canada* - publication of the Canadian Embassy in Mexico, No. 11, 2a. EPOCA - December, 1974, entitled *En La Communicacion Mexico y Canada en el Encuentro Mundial* (Newspaper) Oct. 23-27, 1974.

Interview with Professor McLuhan by Kendig Brubaker Cully and Iris V. Cully, editors of *The Review of Books and Religion*, Vol. 3, No. 9, mid-June, 1974, p. 2 and 15.

"Marshall McLuhan: Double Agent" by George P. Elliott in *The Public Interest,* pp. 116-122 (off-print of this article was sent in on June 20, 1974 - no date or volume number).

*McLuhan Has 'Answers' — Who Has Questions?* in St. Louis University News, Vol. 54, No. 16, Friday, February 7, 1975, page 1 (with photo).

"McLuhan says media ruining mankind" - by Ted Shaw in *Sheridan Sun,* Vol. 5, No. 15, January 9, 1975, p. 1 (Sheridan College - Oakville, Brampton, Mississauga Campuses publication).

"Les Temps Forts De Votre Vie/Suite" by Lila Dubois, Paris correspondent appeared in ELLE magazine, Paris, France, on January 13, 1975.

"McLuhan says we're too shy for transit" - Toronto *Star,* March 26, 1975.

"Car's lost its role" - *Toronto Star,* March 26, 1975 (late edition). (Both of these articles are in reference to remarks made by Prof. McLuhan at the EKISTICS conference held at the City Hall, Toronto, on March 26th). Professor McLuhan replied in a letter to the Editor of the *Star* on March 27/75.

"McLuhan brilliance just too blinding." Letter to the Editor of *The Montreal Star* News and Reviews - by M.P. Scott, Montreal, December 7, 1974.

"McLuhanisms give audience enigmatic food for thought" by Brian Moore - *The Montreal Star,* Sat., November 23, 1974 — re Prof. McLuhan's address to the Provincial Association of Catholic Teachers and the Provincial Association of Protestant Teachers in Montreal.

"Culture Is Our Business" by David E. Ward - *New Zealand Library Association, Otago Branch, Week-End School Proceedings (6 October, 1973)* - Dunedin, New Zealand, 1974. Prof. Ward is in the Dept. of Philosophy at the University of Otago, Dunedin, New Zealand. He wrote his paper at the request of a librarian friend who asked him to 'apply' McLuhan to the Public Library.

"Marshall McLuhan a la 'Conference 75' — Se specialiser? Perime!" article appeared in local newspaper in Montreux, Switzerland after Professor McLuhan's address to "Conference Spectrum Limited" on April 17, 1975. (clipping sent in by W.E. Boehm, Director, Office of Tourism, Montreux).

"Marshall McLuhan in spirited debate with French Critic" — in Toronto *Star*, Friday, May 16, 1975, p. E-6. (Debate with Professor Robert Escarpit, President of the University of Bordeaux, France, took place at the Montreal International Book Fair where Professor McLuhan was one of the principal speakers on May 15th. Theme of the Book Fair was "From Gutenberg to McLuhan").

"Marshall McLuhan Defined: A Transformation From Mosaic to Theoretical Style and Guide to Further Study" — by David J. Brannam. A thesis submitted in partial fulfillment of the requirements for the Degree of Master of Arts in the Department of Speech Communication, California State University, Fresno, Calif. May, 1975.

"McLuhan and Modern Superman" — an interview by Jim Bourret in *The Texas Guardian*, May, 1975, pp. 6 and 8. (This was done while Professor McLuhan was McDermott Distinguished Professor at the University of Dallas from April 10 to May 10, 1975.)

"McLuhan Comments on Electronic Media" — by Dan Frazier — *Fort Worth Star-Telegram*, Friday, April 18, 1975, p. 4-A.

"Marshall McLuhan — Sense or Nonsense?" — by Elaine Viets in *St. Louis Post-Dispatch*, Sunday, Feb. 16, 1975, p. 2-K.

"Guru Is for the Birds" — James Dunlap in *The Dallas Morning News*, Sunday, April 14, 1975, p. 1.

"Big D" — Paul Crume in *Dallas Morning News*, May 5, 1975.

Picture and short comment appeared in *National Geographic* magazine, July, 1975.

"The Media Prophet" — *Newsweek*, Sept. 22, 1975, p. 13.

"It Wouldn't Be So Hard to Take if Toronto Wasn't So Smug About It" by William C. Heine in *The London Free Press*, London, Ont. Friday, Oct. 3, 1975. (Prof. McLuhan mentioned in this article)

"Mind Bombs on the Pacific: The McLuhanesque War to Save the Whales" by Clive Cocking, *Weekend Magazine*, Toronto, September 6, 1975, p. 9.

"Viewpoint: McLuhan as Rorschach" by Samuel L. Becker — *Journal of Broadcasting*. Vol. 19, #2, Spring, 1975, p. 235.

"When Other Lips Stop Moving..." by Wilfred De'Ath - *Hampstead and Highgate Express*, London, England, December 31, 1975 (no page number). Mr. De'Ath is a British free lance journalist who visited the Centre for Culture and Technology and interviewed Professor McLuhan on October 27, 1975.

"English as She Is Not Taught" by Peter Hunt in *The Casket* (National Weekly published in Antigonish, N.S.) Vol. 123, #16, Dec. 4, 1975 — on pages 2 and 3 mentions the work of Professor Marshall McLuhan.

"Marshall McLuhan Is Alive and Well" — Bob Cohen (Southam News Service) *The Windsor Star*, Saturday, October 25, 1975, p. 21.

"Las Organizaciones Estan en Crisis: La Causa: una Deficiente Comunicacion" by Ricardo Medina Macias in *El Diario De Monterrey*, Oct. 30, 1975. Press item about Professor McLuhan's participation in Conference at the Technological Institute of Monterrey, Mexico, on October 29, 1975.

"Why don't I want to live in Calgary?" by Wilfred De'Ath in *The Listener* November 27, 1975, London, England, p. 712.

"Media Get McLuhan Massage" in *Province* (newspaper) — Entertainment Section, October 28, 1975, p. 11 (Vancouver).

"Philosopher of the Global Village: A Dialogue with Marshall McLuhan" by W. Kenneth Richmond — *The Scottish Educational Journal*, Vol. 59, #10, March 12, 1976, pp. 12-13. (published in Edinburgh, Scotland.)

"More Messages from Marshall McLuhan" — *Harvard Magazine*, Vol. 78, #8, (by Melanie Marcus), pp. 58-59. April, 1976.

*IS NOTHING SACRED?* A stage play written and directed by Tom Cooper, on Marshall McLuhan and Harold Innis, took place in the Town Hall, New Innis College, University of Toronto. It ran from April 29th, to May 2, 1976.

"Marshall McLuhan" in *Film* magazine, ul. Pulawska 61, 02-595 Warszawa, p. 10 (Professor McLuhan's comments on 80th Anniversary of Cinema, January issue, 1976).

"FUN stargazes at Marshall McLuhan today!" — *Daily Star* (newspaper) page 1, January 29, 1976. In FUN section, pp. 1, 8 and 9. Hammond, Louisiana, re Professor McLuhan's visit to Southeastern Louisiana University on January 29 and 30, 1976.

"How People Pray" by Victor M. Parachin in *The Catholic Register* February 7, 1976, pp. 1 and 2.

"McLuhan Blasts Electronic Media" — *Future* (published by Florida Technological University, Volume #8, February 27, 1976, #18, page 9. (several photos)

"Une autre maclonerie de J.-C. Germain" — by Angele Dagenais in *Le Devoi*, Montreal, Quebec, January 21, 1976.

"Marshall McLuhan" — *Ecrivains des Ameriques* by Naim Kattan, (chapter in book) Montreal: Editions HMH, 1976, pp. 156-157.

"McLuhan Warns of Apocalypse and Aborts Club's Abortion Debate" by Lynda Hurst, *Toronto Star*, September 30, 1976.

"If the Media Didn't Get Marshall McLuhan's Message in the '60's, Another One Is On The Way" by Barbara Rowes, *People Magazine*, Vol. 6, #12, September 20, 1976, pp. 82-91.

"McLuhan Finds It Tough to Explain Canada" — by David Lazarus, *The Citizen*, Ottawa, Sept. 15, 1976, p. 87.

"Canada Split on its Way" by David Kendall — *The Sunday Sun*, Toronto, May 23, 1976, p. 15.

"Carter Vindicates McLuhan" — by Sander Vanocur — *Rocky Mountain News*, Denver, Colorado, May 11, 1976, p. 44.

Write-up about Professor McLuhan in *Portraits* by Yousuf Karsh, Toronto: Pitt Publishing Company Ltd., 1976, pp. 133-134. Picture on page 135.

Mention of Professor McLuhan is made in "Waiting for the New Order" in *Broadcaster*, March, 1976, p. 24.

Mention of Professor McLuhan in "The Challenge of the Global Village" by Charles Parker in *The Listener*, Vol 96, #2470, August 12, 1976, p. 170.

"The Medium Rebelled Against the Message" — *The Washington Post*, September 26, 1976, p. C7. (Excerpt of conversation between Marshall McLuhan and Tom Brokaw on NBC's *Today Show*, September 24, 1976)

"Pour Une Politique Colturelle Mondiale — un entretien avec McLuhan" par Gilles Plazy et Odile Van de Walle — *Les Nouvelles Litteraires*, September 16, 1976, pp. 2-3. (re UNESCO Symposium on "The Function of Art in Contemporary Life" held in Paris September 6-10, 1976)

"Marshall McLuhan" — an interview by Carl Scharfe in *The Innis Herald*, Innis College, University of Toronto, Vol. 10, #1, October 25, 1976, pp. 3-5 and 9.

1977   "Stones of U of T Tell of Three Great Founders" by Donald Jones, *The Toronto Star*, January 8, 1977, p. B5, an article marking the 150th anniversary of the U of T. Mr. Jones remarks on famous personages at the U of T, past and present (including Professor McLuhan). In detailing historic buildings on the University of Toronto campus, he mentions Professor McLuhan's office: ". . . a small coach house on a back lane that nay one day become the most historic building of them all."

# ADDENDUM

ok   "Marcuse & McLuhan et la nouvelle revolution mondiale" — Jean Marabini. Pref. par Armand Lanoux (Paris, France) Maison Mame, 1973.

ap.   "The Sage of Aquarius: Marshall McLuhan" — Chapter
Book  8 in *The Post-Industrial Prophets: Interpretations of Technology* by William Kuhns. New York: Weybright and Talley, 1971. pp. 169-201.

In *Black Talk* by Ben Sidran, New York: Holt Rinehart, 1971, there is a notation on page xi: "This study owes much to the pioneering work of Marshall McLuhan."

per   "McLuhanist Criticism: Chinatown" — by Peter Dart, U. of Kansas — paper he presented at a recent conference of the Univ. Film Association in Rochester, N.Y. (Prof. Peter Dart, Radio-TV-Film Dept., University of Kansas, Lawrence, Kansas, 66045)

urse   Professor Edison Otero Bello, Departamento de Filosofia, Sede Oriente. University de Chile, Macul 774. Nunoa. Santiago, Chile.

"McLuhan Explains the Evolution of his Methods for Analysing Cultural Change in Relation to Technological Change" — Transcript of an interview by Joseph Foyle made at the Centre for Understanding Media, Leeson Park, Dublin 6, Ireland, Mar. 30, 1972.

"Le Prophete de la Television" — an interview for *L'Express*, Paris, France, done by Gerard Bonnot, Sept. 25, 1967. pp. 83-87.

68   THE (25-page soft-cover booklet) by Barrington Nevitt, based on the theories and insights of Professor McLuhan. Published by Northern Electric Company Ltd., Research and Development Laboratories, Ottawa, Canada.

71   Write-up about Professor McLuhan in *Faces of Our Time* by Yousuf Karsh, Toronto: University of Toronto Press, 1971, pp. 129-130. Picture on page 131.

"The Environmental Surround: An Argument for Resource Centres" by Sam Neill in *British Journal of Educational Technology* Volume 3, #2, May, 1972. References and quotes on pages 73, 141, 151, 152 and 177.

**Thesis** "Christian Communication in the Light of the Theories of Marshall McLuhan" — D.Phil. Dissertation by Raymer B. Matson submitted to the Board of the Faculty of Theology, Oxford University, May, 1967.

"In Defence of McLuhan" by John Chaplin — *ADMAP*, June, 1972, pp. 202-3. (Published by Dorland Advertising Limited, London, England)

**1974** Professor McLuhan quoted in *Colombo's Canadian Quotations*, John R. Colombo, ed., Hurtig Publishers, Edmonton, Alberta, 1974, pp. 396-398.

# DATE DUE

| MAY 24 | | | |
|---|---|---|---|
| | | | |
| | | | |
| | | | |
| | | | |
| | | | |
| | | | |
| | | | |
| | | | |
| | | | |
| | | | |
| | | | |
| | | | |
| | | | |
| | | | |
| | | | |

Demco, Inc. 38-293